The publisher and the University of California Press Foundation gratefully acknowledge the generous support of the Atkinson Family Foundation Imprint in Higher Education.

Is That True?

Is That True?

CRITICAL THINKING FOR SOCIOLOGISTS

Joel Best

UNIVERSITY OF CALIFORNIA PRESS

University of California Press
Oakland, California

© 2021 by Joel Best

Library of Congress Cataloging-in-Publication Data

Names: Best, Joel, author.
Title: Is that true? : critical thinking for sociologists / Joel Best.
Description: Oakland, California : University of California Press, 2021. |
    Includes bibliographical references and index.
Identifiers: LCCN 2020032131 (print) | LCCN 2020032132 (ebook) |
    ISBN 9780520381391 (hardback) | ISBN 9780520381407 (paperback) |
    ISBN 9780520381414 (ebook)
Subjects: LCSH: Critical thinking. | Sociology. | Reasoning.
Classification: LCC B809.2 .B47 2021 (print) | LCC B809.2 (ebook) |
    DDC 160.2/43—dc23
LC record available at https://lccn.loc.gov/2020032131
LC ebook record available at https://lccn.loc.gov/2020032132

Manufactured in the United States of America

25 24 23 22 21
10 9 8 7 6 5 4 3 2 1

Contents

Acknowledgments   *vii*

1. What Is Critical Thinking?   *1*

2. The Basics: Arguments and Assumptions   *8*

3. Everyday Arguments   *14*
   *Anecdotes · Ad Hominem Arguments · Myths · Folk
   Wisdom and Metaphors · Facts · Everyday Reasoning*

4. The Logic of Social Science   *28*
   *Patterns · Causality · Judging Social Scientific Claims · The
   Importance of Evidence*

5. Authority and Social Science Arguments   *39*
   *Challenges for Social Science · The Case of Sociology · Thinking
   about Sociology and Critical Thinking*

6. Sociology as a Social World   *47*
   Camps · Envy · Sociology's Subdivisions

7. Orientations   *60*
   *Optimism and Pessimism · Team Culture and Team
   Structure · Insiders and Outsiders · Tragedy and
   Comedy · The Importance of Orientations*

8. Words   74
    Jargon · Word Fads · Definitions · Concept Creep

9. Questions and Measurements   85
    Sociological Questions · Empirical Questions · Measurement ·
    What Is Being Measured? · Questioning Measurements

10. Variables and Comparison   96
    Variables · Issues with Comparison · Varieties of Comparative
    Findings · Replication · Comparison in Qualitative
    Research · Questioning Comparisons

11. Tendencies   110
    Patterned Tendencies · The Ecological Fallacy · The Modesty
    of Sociological Explanations · Thinking about Tendencies

12. Evidence   119
    Effective Evidence · Not-So-Effective Evidence · Questioning
    Evidence Choices · Questions about Research

13. Echo Chambers   129
    Recognizing and Addressing One's Own Biases · Expectations
    and Sociologists · The Complications of Ideological
    Homogeneity · The Importance of Self-Criticism

14. Tough Topics   140
    Cultural Waves · Good Guys and Bad Guys · Taboos · Thinking
    about What's Difficult

    Afterword: Why Critical Thinking Is Important   151

    Notes   153
    References   159
    Index   165

Acknowledgments

I want to thank the people who spoke with me about this project or looked at various versions of the manuscript and made comments. They include Eric Best, Katie Bogle, Aaron Fichtelberg, Ken Haas, Scott Harris, Jim Holstein, Brian Monahan, Larry Nichols, Dan O'Connell, Diane Pike, Milo Schield, Mac Sommerlatte, and Dave Schweingruber. They made a lot of very helpful suggestions, many of which I adopted, but none of them bear any responsibility for the book's shortcomings. At the University of California Press, I particularly want to thank Naomi Schneider, the sociology editor, and Anne Canright, who copyedited the manuscript.

1 *What Is Critical Thinking?*

Much as politicians endorse motherhood and apple pie, nearly everyone who teaches praises critical thinking.[1] College professors agree that they want their students to become critical thinkers, but so do teachers in lower grades. I've heard first- and second-grade teachers declare that teaching critical thinking was one of their most important jobs. Most educators are with the program.[2]

But we can suspect that when virtually everyone agrees that something is good, they probably define it in different ways. The word *critical* can take on many different meanings. I recall one student recoiling in horror when I spoke positively about critical thinking: "Oh, I don't want to become a *critical* person!" Then there are sociology professors who will boldly declare that they embrace "critical race theory" or "critical animal studies" or . . . you get the idea. Used in this way, *critical* usually signals that their approach is aligned with some sort of liberal/progressive/radical/leftist political perspective. In effect, they use the word *critical* as a sort of brand name to contrast their approach with rival schools of thought that, they charge, support the status quo. While they may assume that adopting a "critical" approach makes them critical thinkers, that's not what I will mean by "critical thinking" here.

Rather, this book views critical thinking as a set of *tools* for evaluating *claims.* A claim is any statement asserting something to be the case. We encounter claims all the time in conversations, in what we read, in the media, indeed, on pretty much every occasion we connect with other people, and we've all had to learn to interpret those claims. We classify claims as being more or less convincing, using terms like *fact* or *information* to identify claims that seem sound, and terms like *rumor* or *fake* to label claims that seem more dubious. Learning to make these distinctions starts early: a lot of parenting involves helping small children become better at evaluating things they hear ("He's only teasing," "I'm really serious," "That's just a story"). At some point, kids have to learn to distinguish between TV programs and the content of commercials, and to understand that advertisers' claims may not be completely truthful. As we get older, we learn that flattery and compliments might not reveal what others actually are thinking, just as most of us learn to discount rival claims made during election campaigns. We learn to distinguish questionable claims from others that seem more likely to be true.

The ability to think critically is important. Imagine a person incapable of critical thinking: this would be someone so suggestible (and vulnerable) that he or she takes every commercial's advice to rush out and buy the product being advertised, and finds every politician convincing. Obviously, few people are that weak. Yet while becoming skeptical or suspicious of what we're told by people who want to sell us something is a useful skill, it isn't enough. We constantly encounter claims in news stories, books, and articles; from radio, television, and online personalities; in blog posts, podcasts, downloaded videos, and social media. How are we to evaluate all these claims? How can we separate ones that probably can be accepted as true from those that we should doubt?

People have different standards for making these judgments. One popular standard throughout history has been to assume that [we already know what is true]—that there is some sacred book that contains all the truths we need to know and that we can simply judge all claims by whether they are consistent with this holy writ. Or that some great thinker—Aristotle, say, or Confucius, or Marx—already explained how the world works, and we can evaluate today's claims in terms of how well they match those classic interpretations. Assuming you already know what's right and true can be comforting, if only because it justifies ignoring those who hold different views. Anyone who has ever gotten into an argument about religion knows that people who believe some sort of authoritative doctrine are hard to budge.

This book presents critical thinking as a more modest, alternative approach for assessing claims. Instead of simply assuming that we already know what is true, critical thinking requires that we consider the possibility that our assumptions might be wrong. At bottom, *critical thinking is about evidence.* Evidence is information that can help us judge whether a claim is true. When we hear a claim, we ought to evaluate the evidence for and against it. The claim may be about something small and personal ("I love your hair in that style") or aimed at a much larger audience (today's top news story). It doesn't matter. Thinking critically involves examining the evidence for a claim and deciding whether it is convincing. When this book refers to "critical thinking," then, it will mean ways of weighing evidence and distinguishing between stronger evidence and weaker evidence.

This sort of critical thinking has a history. It began to catch on during the Enlightenment—the centuries-long movement refuting the idea that all truth could be found in the Bible or Aristotle.

Instead, people started collecting and evaluating observable facts and information—i.e., evidence. For instance, they used telescopes to make observations of the planets and stars, and what they saw convinced them that the earth revolved around the sun, thus contradicting theologians' insistence that the earth was the center of the universe. Later, they used microscopes to identify tiny organisms that seemed to cause diseases, which led medical authorities to reluctantly reject Aristotle's model of disease being caused by an imbalance of the body's four humors. These were tough debates: some theologians and physicians never stopped resisting the new ideas. But today, those pieces of evidence have won out: most people accept that the earth orbits the sun, and that germs can lead to disease. Yet we continue to argue about plenty of other things. Most people now agree that evidence is important, even though they may disagree about what the evidence shows.

Critical thinking in the sense of weighing evidence is a skill. It can be learned, and one gets better at it with practice. Perhaps you're surprised that so many educators agree that teaching critical thinking is important. After all, your high school probably didn't offer classes in critical thinking. You took classes in mathematics or science, language or literature, and social studies or history. Still, your teachers probably thought that all those classes were teaching critical thinking skills: math taught you to perform mathematical reasoning, literature classes involved analyzing plays and poetry, history encouraged you to assess different explanations of key events, and so on. Those lessons were designed to teach you something about the substance of math, literature, and history, but they were also intended to make you a more critical thinker, someone who not only knew something about the subjects in question, but also could apply the analytic skills those lessons taught to a variety of topics and contexts.

Learning to think critically is a major reason why there is a strong correlation between level of education and income: on average, high school graduates earn more than those who drop out; people with some college make more than those who don't go beyond high school; those who graduate from college earn a lot more than those who don't receive a degree; and people who go on to finish graduate or professional degrees make more than college graduates. Why should this be true? Lots of high school and college classes don't seem directly relevant to most jobs. But the subject matter covered in those classes is less important than acquiring the critical thinking skills students need to succeed in college. A college graduate should have learned to read thoughtfully enough to comprehend difficult material, to locate information and evaluate its quality, and to develop, organize, and present their own reasoned arguments. By completing coursework—doing the assigned reading, studying for tests, writing term papers, and so on—students develop and use increasingly sophisticated critical thinking skills. At bottom, it is those relatively rare and valuable skills that qualify better-educated individuals for higher-paying jobs.

In other words, while the term *critical thinking* may seem vague, abstract, or impractical, it is actually the key to education. Consider a question sometimes posed to grade-school children: "There are 125 sheep and 5 dogs in a flock. How old is the shepherd?"[3] Mathematics educators note that most children facing this question assume they must be being asked to produce a number, such as 25 (125 divided by 5). After all, arithmetic students constantly confront "word problems" that require them to calculate the correct numeric answer. But the shepherd question does not give us any information relevant to solving the problem; neither the number of sheep nor the number of dogs has any bearing on the shepherd's age. The correct answer is that there is no way of knowing how old the shepherd is. Arriving at that answer involves critical thinking—assessing whether the information available is sufficient to answer the question. Another way of saying this is that education is supposed to teach students to distinguish sense from nonsense. In the end, critical thinking is an extremely practical set of skills.

There are lots of ways to evaluate evidence, and different disciplines tend to emphasize different critical thinking skills.[4] This book discusses critical thinking for sociologists. Why sociology? Well, for starters, I am a sociologist, so it is what I know, study, and teach. There are lots of books that approach critical thinking in very general terms. Many of them are written by philosophers, and I tend to find them awfully abstract. I am less interested in grand theoretical principles for critical thinking than in understanding how practicing sociologists might think more critically.

In particular, this book focuses on thinking critically about arguments made by sociologists and other social scientists about social issues. Very simply, social science involves doing research—identifying, collecting, and assessing evidence from our social world—to better understand social life. The arguments that social scientists make based on this research attempt to explain how and why people behave in the ways they do, and how that behavior can aggravate (or reduce) social problems. Not all explanations for social behavior involve social scientific reasoning. For instance, some people might explain crime by saying that "people are born to sin" (an argument grounded in particular religious teachings), but that claim doesn't strike sociologists as terribly useful because it is not a testable social scientific proposition. What *is* a testable proposition? That is something we will be exploring in these pages.

Because I am a sociologist, a lot of my examples are going to involve sociological topics, but most of what I have to say is applicable to other social scientific approaches. This includes the social scientific parts of other academic disciplines, such as anthropology, communications, criminology, economics, geography, history, political science, and psychology, as well as various interdisciplinary "studies" programs, including area studies (such as African studies or East Asian studies), ethnic studies (such as black studies and chicano/latino studies), and women's studies. Social scientific arguments also sometimes appear in various applied disciplines that involve professionals working with clients, often located in schools of business, education, law, medicine, public policy, and social work.

In all of these disciplines, there are people trying to understand social life scientifically—that is, to explain patterns in people's behavior based on evidence. The resulting arguments are important because they often are used to justify social policies that affect lots of people. Therefore, we need to be able to think critically about these arguments. But before we can focus on how sociologists think, we need to consider how arguments work.

Critical Thinking Takeaway

- Critical thinking involves evaluating arguments by weighing the evidence that supports them.

2 The Basics

Arguments and Assumptions

In this book, [the word *argument* simply means an attempt to persuade, a line of reasoning with one or more claims that lead to a conclusion.] An argument doesn't need to be dramatic, or hostile. If John says, "Since it is raining right now and we don't want to get wet, I think we should delay going outside until it stops," he is making an argument. The argument consists of *grounds* that provide basic information (it is raining), *warrants* that justify drawing some conclusion (we don't want to get wet), and the *conclusion* itself (therefore, we should stay inside and wait for the rain to stop).[1]

Critical thinking refers to evaluating or assessing an argument to see whether it is convincing. For example, when considering John's argument, you might ask whether it is still raining, whether it is raining hard enough to make going outside uncomfortable, whether you actually care about getting wet, or whether you have some urgent reason for going outside now that makes getting wet seem unimportant. Depending on the answers, you might agree that the argument is convincing and choose to stay indoors, or you might consider the argument unpersuasive and decide to risk heading out.

[handwritten margin note: arguments are not always negative]

Because all arguments consist of grounds, warrants, and conclusions, thinking critically requires evaluating each of these elements. Grounds statements are claims about the way things are. In John's argument, the grounds are the straightforward claim that it is raining right now. We can evaluate this claim by looking outside to check whether it really is raining, or perhaps we might get into a discussion about just how hard it's raining, or about what "raining" actually means—is it just misting or sprinkling or lightly raining, and is that enough precipitation to make us want to stay indoors? Other claims ("Poverty is caused by discrimination and other problematic social arrangements," say, or "Poverty is caused by a culture that discourages effort") may be supported by all sorts of more complicated evidence—examples, statistics, definitions, and so on—and there are various ways of approaching such grounds statements. Do the statements *seem* true? Do we have enough evidence to *evaluate* the statements? Does the evidence seem strong, or does it have weaknesses? Are there other things we'd like to know? And so on. Arguments may have elaborate grounds consisting of several statements, and there may be lots of reasons to criticize those grounds.

Warrants are justifications; they invoke values. The warrant that we don't want to get wet justifies John's conclusion. Thinking about warrants can be tricky. Sometimes, warrants are implicit: if the person making the argument and the people who hear it share the same values, it may not seem necessary to spell out the argument's warrants. That is, John might assume that no one wants to get wet if they can avoid it, and so not bother stating the warrant, but simply say, "Since it is raining right now, I think we should delay going outside until it stops." Criticizing warrants can be uncomfortable because it might draw attention to fundamental disagreements if the critic is advocating for values that are different from those held by the individual making the argument. Still, warrants are essential elements in any argument, and like grounds, they can be critically evaluated. Grounds and warrants form the basis for the argument's conclusion, their purpose may be signaled by words like *because* or *since* (as in our example: "*Since* it is raining right now . . . ").

Finally, an argument's conclusion is presented as the logical result of the grounds plus warrants. Sometimes, words such as *so* or *therefore* mark the conclusion; in other cases, this is implicit. Or we can frame the argument as an *if . . . then* assertion: *If* we can agree that it is raining and that we don't want to get wet, *then* we arrive at the conclusion that we should stay inside. But it is also possible to criticize an argument's conclusion, to point to reasons why the conclusion needn't follow. Maybe this is an emergency (we are out of ice cream!) and we *need* to go outside even in pouring rain; or perhaps we have enough umbrellas and rain gear that we can stay comfortably dry. While those making arguments often suggest that theirs is the only possible conclusion, it nonetheless may be possible to offer critical comments about conclusions, as well as grounds and warrants.

I've borrowed the grounds-warrants-conclusions framework from *The Uses of Argument* by the philosopher Stephen Toulmin. There is a long history of philosophers trying to understand arguments; they usually write about two subjects: rhetoric and logic. Rhetoric is the study of persuasion, understanding how and why arguments seem convincing. For example, was John's pointing out that it was raining enough to convince us to stay indoors, or could the claim be altered to make the argument seem more compelling—by, say, John asserting not just that "it's raining," but that "it's pouring down rain"? Logic, in turn, attempts to evaluate the strength of arguments, whether the grounds and warrants are sufficient to convince someone who is thinking rationally to accept the argument's conclusions. Logicians (the philosophers who study logic) identify logical fallacies—flawed forms of argument in which the conclusion does not necessarily follow. (We will have more to say about fallacies in later chapters.)

Every argument depends on assumptions. Often these are unstated parts of grounds or warrants that are taken for granted. This need not cause concern. We routinely assume, for instance, that gravity is in play, and the people we're talking to doubtless agree (unless our subject happens to be outer space). But there are plenty of assumptions that can cause mischief.

When you talk to someone who holds very different religious beliefs or political opinions than you do, disagreement is to be expected. A conversation about religion between someone who confidently believes that God exists and another who simply does not is likely to end up with them talking past each other. Not only is each making a critical assumption that the other does not accept, but each may take his or her own assumption for granted, not realizing that it is just that: an assumption. It can be hard for us to even recognize our own assumptions, and of course it is hard to think critically about them because—after all—we are already convinced they are true.

Assumptions are necessary to argument, however. We can't be expected to supply the entire chain of reasoning (about gravity, for example) that leads to every claim we make. At the same time, we need to acknowledge that we do make assumptions, and be prepared to explain and defend them when they are questioned.

It tends to be much trickier to think critically about arguments made by people with whom you agree than it is to criticize the arguments of those who hold views you don't share. When confronted with a view we don't share, we find it easy to pick apart the argument and identify its flawed assumptions and reasoning. Meanwhile, claims by those who share our views may get a pass. Maybe, we tell ourselves, their argument isn't perfect, maybe the evidence is a little weak or the logic a little flawed, but we shouldn't be too critical because, at bottom, we agree that these people are right. This is an issue that will reappear at several points in the chapters that follow.

If it is hard to think critically about arguments made by people with whom we agree, it is even tougher to criticize arguments that we make ourselves. It is easy to develop a kind of selective blindness to our own sloppy thinking. It is also dangerous: because if we don't think critically about our own arguments, others will find it easy to challenge our claims. Far better that we inspect our arguments, consider their limitations, and address those problems *before* we present them to other people. We should try to make our reasoning, if not bulletproof, at least as difficult to criticize as possible. *In many ways, then, the most important form of critical thinking is the thought that we apply to our own ideas, allowing us to address whatever problems we spot in our reasoning.*

All critical thinking involves evaluating grounds, warrants, and conclusions. This is not as simple as it seems, for there are lots of ways to make these evaluations. Although this book is going to focus largely on arguments made by sociologists and other social scientists it will help to begin by examining the sorts of arguments we encounter in everyday situations.

Critical Thinking Takeaways

- All arguments contain grounds, warrants, conclusions, and assumptions. Critical thinking involves assessing these elements.
- It is easiest to think critically about arguments when you disagree, harder when you agree, and hardest when you are the one making the argument.

3   *Everyday Arguments*

Lots of us enjoy discussing—even debating—different aspects of society. Anything from the latest news headline to a walk through our neighborhood can inspire such a conversation. An opinion is uttered, someone else chimes in to either agree or disagree, and we're off.

These conversations tend to be relaxed, without many rules about what you can or can't contribute. The arguments that people make—with their grounds, warrants, and conclusions—receive little close scrutiny. As a result, there are no clear standards for what we might call critical thinking in these situations.

This chapter examines some common elements of everyday arguments that are flawed. They are tempting to use, and may even seem convincing on the surface, but they have limitations that need to be understood.

Anecdotes

Arguments often feature stories about one's own experiences: "Just the other day I saw. . . . " Usually these tales are intended to provide firsthand evidence of something that the speaker means to be understood as common, or a particular example offered as support for some broader claim: "I saw two people sitting at a table in a restaurant, each of them staring at their own phone. We are losing the ability to talk to one another face-to-face."

In other cases, the anecdote is not firsthand. Instead, the teller relays a story that he or she heard from a friend or on the news. But again, the implication is that this case is somehow typical. Thus, an example of someone who fraudulently claimed benefits from a social welfare program can be used to argue that many of the program's beneficiaries do not really need or deserve assistance.[1]

Such anecdotes may seem quite compelling to the people telling them, but they should not be considered especially strong evidence. The very fact that a story is distinctive or memorable enough to catch your attention may be a sign that this case is not at all typical. A single example (for instance, you know a poor person who strikes you as lazy) is a weak basis for broad generalizations (all poor people are lazy). After all, we occupy a big world with billions of people living all sorts of lives. A story about something we have witnessed can no more represent the complexity of the whole world than any one photograph can depict everything we might see. Even if someone can regale us with two or three or even more examples, we need to realize that we all travel in more or less restricted social circumstances. Let's say Sally, a teacher we know, complains about bad behavior among some of her students. Perhaps she can offer lots of examples, perhaps she convinces us that the students in her classroom are indeed a difficult bunch. How confident can we be that her experiences with her class tell us much about what's going on in other classrooms, or in other schools?

Anecdotes are almost inevitably about atypical or unusual behavior—something that caught the teller's attention and seemed interesting enough to share with others. After driving through traffic, we aren't likely to tell anyone about all the other drivers we witnessed stopping at red lights; it is the driver who ran the red light who becomes the anecdote.

Suppose Carlos tells you he saw just such a red-light-running driver, then declares, "Traffic is getting more and more dangerous with drivers like that on the roads." If you check the statistics collected by traffic enforcement agencies, though, you will find that in fact rates of traffic fatalities have fallen dramatically over the last several decades.[2] Obviously, this doesn't mean that Carlos didn't see someone run a red light; but it might make us question his conclusion that that red-light-running driver proves that today's roadways are more dangerous than they used to be.

Of course, if you remark that traffic fatality rates are down, Carlos might respond that such statistics are irrelevant: after all, no one died when the driver he saw ran that red light. This raises an important point about evidence. Evidence is almost never complete or perfect. There is no way of knowing the precise rate at which drivers run red lights; we can't monitor every driver's approach to every stop light, and even if we could, we can't go back in time to make similar measurements, so we can't possibly prove that red light running has increased (or, for that matter, declined). So we look for the *best available* evidence. We might assume that, in contrast to fender benders, many of which may never come to the attention of law enforcement, accidents serious enough to cause a fatality are almost sure to be reported, and as a result, counts of traffic fatalities are probably reasonably accurate. So, it is not unreasonable to counter Carlos's anecdote about the driver who ran a red light with evidence that traffic fatality rates are declining. Presumably if reckless driving is becoming more common, accidents should be increasing, and so should fatalities.

It is certainly possible to continue to debate the value of the traffic fatality evidence. Carlos might suggest, for example, that increased recklessness may be causing a big rise in nonfatal accidents. But without more evidence to support that claim, his argument has no teeth. The point here is that evidence is key to a successful argument.

Anecdotes have another feature: they usually describe a sequence of events—Q happened, and then R followed, and that led to S. It is important to appreciate that such stories or narratives have their own limitations. Any narrative is necessarily selective; it is impossible to tell a tale that encompasses everything that happened. Highlighting the Q-R-S sequence inevitably ignores A through P.

One way to think critically about a narrative is to question its choice of elements. Have all the relevant events been included? Are parts of the narrative's sequence irrelevant? That is, does it make better sense to add elements (to tell the story as P-Q-R-S, instead of just Q-R-S), or even to subtract some (so that we have only Q-S)? Disagreements about why something happened—anything from how we wound up eating at this restaurant to whether slavery caused the Civil War—often revolve around which elements are selected to make sense of the story.

Even when we agree about the essential elements in the story, we may interpret them differently. When Carlos tells the tale of the red light runner, he suggests that the driver was simply reckless, but a critic might propose other possible explanations: perhaps the driver had an emergency or whatever. Agreeing on the relevant elements in a sequence does not necessarily mean that people will agree on an interpretation. Notice that we may be inclined to accept some stories that fit well with our ideas of what is relevant or true and resist others because they seem to contradict what we believe.

We all use anecdotes. Stories can make things seem clearer, which is why authors and journalists often begin their books and news stories with an example so as to give their topic a human dimension. But anecdotes have limitations. If someone making a sweeping declaration—"The world is going to hell!"—is asked for evidence—"What makes you say that?"—and responds with an anecdote, about people looking at their cellphones or running a red light, say, at first glance this simple evidence may seem sufficient to support the conclusion. But an anecdote is always weak, imperfect, incomplete as evidence. We ought to try to move beyond specific examples if we want to understand social life.

Ad Hominem Arguments

An ad hominem argument is one that focuses on the person who has said something, rather than on what has been said. Claiming, "Well, that person is an environmentalist [or a conservative or _____ just fill in the blank], so I don't have to listen" rejects the message because it comes from a particular messenger. This is dangerous, because it closes off the listener from whatever ideas that person may be presenting.

Of course, people disagree about lots of things. But it is a mistake to think that you can simply ignore or reject out of hand whatever the people you disagree with might say. It is fine to reject an argument because of its weaknesses, but not simply because it was made by a kind of person with whom you probably disagree.

It can be tempting to fall into ad hominem arguments. Most of us have complex identities that include particular political or religious views, and we know that others disagree with those views. People who consider themselves liberals realize that other folks think of themselves as conservatives, and vice versa. We probably can sketch rough descriptions of what people on the other side of the fence think, and we probably find their arguments predictable; we may think we already know what they are going to say. Still, to ignore argument simply because the person making it belongs to a category of people who disagree with us is an error of reasoning.

The term *ad hominem* is Latin, meaning "to the person"; the error involves addressing the supposed motivations or biases of the person making an argument, while ignoring the argument's intrinsic logic or evidence. It is a logical fallacy that was named centuries ago, at a time when learned people wrote their analyses in Latin.[3]

The key to critical thinking is assessing evidence. Assessing does not mean accepting. As we have already noted, there is nothing wrong with arguing that an anecdote is a relatively weak form of evidence, that a description of a specific incident is a poor basis for making broad generalizations. But that is not at all the same as rejecting the anecdote's relevance because the person telling the story holds beliefs different from yours.

Intense conflicts often lead opponents to develop dismissive, hostile names for one another—slurs based on ethnicity, religion, or politics. These labels are hurled back and forth, and they encourage ad hominem critiques: if Jane is a [derogatory label], then we don't need to listen to her ideas or even to her evidence—whether that's the evidence she presents in support of her own claims or in her critiques of our arguments. This is a seductive line of thinking because it seems to excuse us from taking our opponent seriously.

And it returns us to the familiar temptation: simply to criticize our opponent's arguments (or just ignore them), as opposed to the much more challenging task of thinking critically about what we ourselves are claiming in response. Ad hominem arguments are terribly dangerous, because they cause us to huddle among those who share our views, while discouraging us from using our capacity to engage in critical thinking.

While this chapter is focused on pitfalls in everyday argument, we will have occasion to further discuss ad hominem arguments in later chapters dealing with sociological reasoning.

Myths

Like ad hominem critiques, calling something a "myth" is another way to justify dismissing an argument out of hand, without considering its merits. Folklorists—the people who actually study myths—use the term to refer to origin tales about gods and goddesses and how the world took form. Different cultures have different myths—the Greeks and Romans, the Norse people, and the Navajo: all have their own mythologies. In everyday conversation, however, calling something a myth is to argue that it is false, and that only mistaken people believe it. Presumably the reasoning is that since we consider tales featuring Aphrodite or Thor as fictional, the key feature of these myths must be that they are not true. Social scientists sometimes use the term this way. For example, one can find lists of rape myths—sets of statements about rape that some people may believe but that, the analysts insist, are simply false (e.g., "Women incite men to rape," "Women fantasize about being raped"). Similarly, there are lists of marriage myths, disaster myths, immigration myths, and so on.

As we have seen, there is nothing wrong with reviewing the evidence regarding some claim and arguing that that evidence is so weak that the claim should be rejected. It is less clear that labeling such claims as myths is helpful. Calling a claim a myth dismisses it, simply by declaring it to be false: "Some people believe that X happens, but that isn't true; it's just a myth." But what does this mean? Is the argument that it is a myth because X never happens, or that it happens only infrequently, or what? Much like ad hominem arguments, the myth label promotes dismissing an argument out of hand without actually assessing its evidence.

This is a tactic that can be used by anyone who wants to challenge particular ideas. Try Googling global warming myths or inequality myths—or virtually any social issue + *myth*. All of these folks are using the term *myth* to say, in effect, that some misguided people may believe X, but X is just wrong, wrong, wrong.

Notice, too, that people with competing views often declare the other side's assertions to be myths. Thus, a *Huffington Post* piece entitled "10 Abortion Myths That Need To Be Busted" begins: "1. MYTH: Abortion is dangerous"; while "10 Pro-Abortion Myths That Need to Be Completely Debunked," an article posted on *LifeNews.com,* leads off with "1. MYTH: Abortion is safe."[4] Or take competing lists about guns: the second myth discussed in the *Federalist's* "7 Gun Control Myths That Just Won't Die" is "Nobody's Demanding Gun Confiscation"; yet "10 Pro-Gun Myths, Shot Down," from *Mother Jones,* features as Myth #1: "They're coming for your guns."[5] Such examples of contradictory myth-spotting suggest that simply branding claims as false—or as myths—may be overly simplistic.

We can suspect that it would help to define some of these terms. What precisely do these folks mean by "safe," "dangerous," "confiscation," or "coming for"? These claims to identify myths seem to argue for a kind of absolutism: if something isn't completely true, then it must be absolutely false. Clarifying definitions may resolve some of this confusion. Take abortion—is it safe or is it dangerous? One approach might be to acknowledge that abortion is a medical procedure, and that every medical procedure carries risk that something might go wrong. We can, however, suspect that the vast majority of abortions performed by doctors—like the vast majority of, say, appendectomies—do not lead to serious medical complications, and still agree that some very small number of abortions may result in problems.[6] Perhaps the issue is not whether abortion is perfectly safe (in the sense that no woman who undergoes abortion ever suffers harm), but whether it is relatively safe in the sense that other well-established medical procedures that rarely lead to harm are considered safe. This definition might lead us to argue that abortion is about as safe as other common medical treatments. On the other hand, a different definition—say, that any evidence of harm having occurred justifies considering abortion risky—might lead to acknowledgment that it and lots of other medical procedures involve some danger. Understanding either claim requires that we examine both the definitions being used and the evidence; we can't simply impose the word *myth* and consider the matter settled.

But examining the evidence is precisely what calling something a myth discourages. Giving reasons why a particular belief may or may not hold up to scrutiny is a form of critical thinking, but simply responding to a claim with "That's a myth" is, in effect, an argument that there is no need for reasoning, that the matter is settled. Critical thinking demands that we review the evidence. This will not necessarily end debate—reasonable people may still disagree about how to interpret the evidence; but at least it offers a more solid basis for discussion.

Folk Wisdom and Metaphors

In addition to studying myths, some folklorists study aphorisms—those little sayings that are invoked to support everyday arguments. Aphorisms are often contradictory. Imagine a conversation where Bob says he's having difficulty making a decision regarding work. Maria urges him on by remarking, "He who hesitates is lost." But then Vince adds, "Look before you leap." These two time-worn bits of advice advocate opposite courses of action, and probably won't be of much use to Bob. In other words, folk wisdom tends to be awfully flexible: it is usually possible to drag out some aphorism to support whatever argument one wants to make.

A related form of talk is the invocation of metaphors. The course that Bob says he's considering taking may sound on the surface reasonable, but Vince might comment, "Sounds like a slippery slope to me," or remarks that it could be just the tip of the iceberg, meaning, respectively, that making a small concession now will inevitably lead to further concessions, or that whatever is visible may be only a small part of the whole. Metaphors can make conversations more colorful, at least until they become so overly familiar that people dismiss them as clichés. But their real purpose is to condense a larger argument into a single, familiar bit of folk wisdom.

The problem with metaphors is that they can discourage thinking critically about the claim being made. We all know that only the tip of the iceberg, about 10 percent of the whole, is above the waterline and visible. When the metaphor is used to describe, say, some social issue, we are being asked to imagine a hidden, vastly larger problem that would have to be addressed eventually. Of course, that may be true; there probably are some cases where we simply can't see the underlying issues. But what proportion is hidden? Is it really 90 percent (as in the case of a real iceberg's hidden mass)? Or is it only 50 percent? Or significantly less? Without presenting anything in the way of evidence, the iceberg metaphor encourages us to imagine that the issue is much larger than it may in fact be.

Aphorisms and metaphors are verbal shortcuts; they package strings of reasoning into just a few, familiar words. This is valuable, even necessary.[7] Imagine how sluggish our thinking would be if we could not use metaphorical reasoning to recognize similarities and act on them. Yet because they simplify complexity, metaphors can also easily misdirect us. We need to think critically about where they are leading us and whether that's where we want to go.

Facts

Our commonsense understanding of fact is that it refers to something that is simply true. The declaration "That's just a fact!" is often intended as a kind of argumentative trump card—a statement that cannot be disputed. At the same time, we know that people sometimes get into arguments over just what the facts are. How is this possible?

A better way to think about facts is to realize that facts depend on social agreement. Imagine a gathering of people who belong to a particular religion, who all agree a particular book is holy, that it is the word of God. Within that gathering of believers, people may agree that it is a "fact" that that book reveals God's will. Now, suppose other people with different beliefs join the gathering; perhaps they don't believe in God, or perhaps they believe that a different book reveals God's will. Suddenly there is going to be disagreement among those present about what is factual.

This example demonstrates that facts are social; they depend on people agreeing about the evidence—and those agreements can change. Today, small children learn that the earth is one of eight planets that revolve around the sun in our solar system; this is taught as a fact. When I was in school, though, I was taught that there were nine planets. And a thousand years ago, people were confident that the sun revolved around the earth–this was considered a fact. Similarly, in seventeenth-century Massachusetts, people considered the existence of witches to be a fact; today we dismiss that belief as ridiculous. We explain these changes in what is considered factual in terms of improvements in people's understanding of the evidence; this allows us to dismiss earlier factual claims as erroneous.

What is deemed factual can also vary from group to group. Whether it is considered a fact that a particular book is the actual word of God depends on whom you ask. A group of believers may affirm it as a fact, but a collection of people with more diverse religious beliefs will not necessarily agree.

Senator Daniel Patrick Moynihan (who was a social scientist before he entered politics) reportedly said, "Everyone is entitled to his own opinion, but not to his own facts." This reveals our commonsense understanding that two contradictory statements cannot both be factual. This is why the expression "alternative facts" quickly became a target of ridicule. Critical thinking requires that, when we are confronted with two antithetical claims, we weigh the evidence. But there are other, less critically satisfying responses, such as announcing that because you know that what your group believes is true, anyone who says something different is wrong.

Weighing the evidence will not necessarily lead to immediate agreement on what the facts are. People may question another's evidence or the way that evidence is interpreted. People who hold strong beliefs often cling to what they believe, even in the face of evidence that strikes others as compelling. The historical record is filled with cases where people believed prophecies that the end of the world was nigh. So far, all of those predictions have proved wrong, and yet most true believers continued to hold to their convictions.[8] Nor is the tendency to cling to discredited theories limited to religious believers. Scientists have been known to be slow to accept findings that seemed to discredit their positions.[9]

We like to think that the facts are the facts, that they are true, a sort of last word that cannot be disputed. But what is considered factual always reflects some social consensus: at some particular time, there is agreement among some specific people that something is true. Critical thinking is a tool that can help us sort through evidence for and against claims that something is factual. We may conclude that that evidence supports the consensus, that we can agree that a claim that something is a fact is well founded; but we also need to understand that claiming that something is a fact is not, in and of itself, enough to end debate.

Everyday Reasoning

Critical thinking is something we all do, every day. We argue with one another about such everyday matters as our tastes in music, food, sports, and politics. Disagreeing with others, standing up for our own ideas, or being persuaded by someone else's arguments can be fun; or we can agree to disagree, even tease those we disagree with about their preferences. Most of these discussions are casual and not very consequential, so we don't worry too much about the quality of the reasoning. But sometimes disagreements grow heated, and we become frustrated when others don't accept our reasoning. As this chapter has tried to point out, mundane reasoning can be flawed, and it can help if we are able to examine it critically.

We can be pretty good about thinking critically in the context of everyday arguments, at least when we care enough to disagree. Listen to two people debating the relative merits of their favorite quarterbacks or their favorite television shows, and you can find them offering up evidence to support their own positions and criticizing the evidence for the other side. But in other cases, when we already agree with one another or when we just don't care very much, we may not bother thinking critically about the evidence. We just nod along with an anecdote or ignore ad hominem attacks.

That said, when flawed arguments spill over into serious attempts to understand the world, critical thinking becomes very important. The efforts of social scientists trying to improve our understanding of social life, for example, merit critical evaluation. This is the subject of the remaining chapters.

Critical Thinking Takeaways

- Anecdotes are a weak form of evidence.
- Ad hominem arguments and dismissing claims as "myths" are ways of avoiding critical thinking.
- Aphorisms and metaphors may contain assumptions that need inspection.
- Facts depend on social agreement.

4 *The Logic of Social Science*

The goal of science is to better understand the world. Scientific claims are evaluated by a particular set of standards: we make observations of the world to acquire evidence for a claim; any claims inconsistent with that evidence are rejected.

The social sciences seek to apply these scientific standards to understanding human behavior. This means that for sociologists and other social scientists, critical thinking centers on evaluating evidence and the resulting explanations about how people behave.

Patterns

Social science begins with trying to recognize patterns in social life. These patterns vary. Some are easy to spot: men cannot bear children, only women can do so. Others are harder to recognize. Do students who sit near the front of a classroom earn better grades than those who sit in the back? We might suspect this could be true; but we can also imagine that not all students sitting near the front receive particularly high grades, just as some students sitting near the back do really well. Still, we might predict that there will be a *tendency* for those who sit near the front to receive higher grades—that is, that there will be a pattern.

[If we want to go beyond speculating that this pattern might exist, however, we'll need to gather evidence, both to confirm to ourselves that our prediction is correct and to convince others.] We could, for example, keep track of where students sit in a particular class, then check their grades. But even if our hypothesis is confirmed and we find that students who sat near the front tended to receive higher grades, other people might challenge our finding—arguing, for instance, that evidence from that one class hardly proves that the same pattern will be found in all classes. Such challenges are a form of critical thinking, and most research will face such critiques. As we will see in later chapters, deciding how to gather the best evidence can be complicated.

Causality Precedence, patterned variation, rationale, nonspuriness nonspuriousness

Identifying a pattern is not enough. People are likely to ask *why* that particular pattern exists: they will want an explanation for the pattern. Explanations involve an argument that a certain cause produces a certain effect. Basically, every causal argument has to meet four criteria.[1] The names given to these criteria vary, but it is important to understand what each involves.

Precedence

[The first and simplest criterion is precedence: the cause has to occur before the effect.] In our example, where students sit in the classroom occurs first, and the grades they receive come later. So we can say that it is at least plausible that where students sit *may* influence—be at least part of the cause—for the grades they receive.

Notice that it would make no sense to argue that the grades students received after the class ended caused them to sit where they did when the class met. This probably seems obvious, but even distinguished researchers occasionally make this error. For instance, Howard S. Becker, a very fine sociologist, argued that Congress passed the Marihuana Tax Act of 1937 (the original federal law prohibiting marijuana) after the Federal Bureau of Narcotics waged a public relations campaign that led major magazines to publish articles about the drug's dangers. These articles then aroused public opinion, which led to pressure on Congress to pass the bill. In presenting evidence to support his argument, Becker noted that the *Reader's Guide to Periodical Literature* (in those days the leading index for articles in popular magazines) showed that coverage of marijuana peaked in the index volume covering July 1937–June 1939: there were seventeen articles about marijuana indexed in that volume of the *Reader's Guide,* whereas no other volume of the index between 1925 and 1951 listed more than 4 articles. Presumably those magazine articles must have helped inspire the public concern that led to the bill's passage in July 1937.[2]

While at first Becker's argument might seem persuasive, Donald T. Dickson looked more carefully at the dates when the magazine articles were published and noted that "no articles appeared in the five months preceding the House committee hearings on the act in late April and early May, one appeared in July, 1937, and the rest appeared after the bill was signed into law on August 2, 1937."[3] In other words, what Becker identified as a cause— magazine articles that supposedly aroused the public to demand

Congress take action—actually occurred after the supposed effect (the act's passage). In this case, the criterion of precedence is violated.[4]

In many cases, precedence cannot be established by something as clear-cut as the publication dates of magazine articles. In practice, precedence can be complicated by *feedback:* that is, X may influence Y, but then Y proceeds to influence X. This can lead to complicated chicken-or-egg debates about, for instance, whether culture precedes and thereby causes particular social structures to emerge, or whether social structure precedes and similarly causes particular cultures to develop.

Patterned Variation

[This is a relatively straightforward idea: there needs to be a pattern between the cause and effect.] If I flip the light switch up and the light goes on—or down, and it goes off—this pattern makes it reasonable to suspect that flipping the switch causes the light to turn on or off. That is, our cause and effect need to vary in a patterned way. Of course, causal patterns often are not so straightforward. We probably won't find that course grades are perfectly correlated with where students sit in our classroom, such that all of the students with high grades are sitting closest to the front, and so on. Rather, we are likely to find that students sitting toward the front are somewhat more likely to get higher grades—they tend to do better. Similarly, researchers find that smokers are more likely to develop various diseases than nonsmokers, even though some smokers don't get sick and some nonsmokers do. In the real world, patterned variation involves tendencies—the cause makes it more likely that the effect will occur. Identifying and evaluating such patterns often requires using statistics that measure the likelihood that some possible cause shapes the effect.

Rationale

The third criterion for establishing causality involves our ability to explain why the cause ought to shape the effect. Thus, I might explain that flipping the light switch up closes an electrical circuit, which causes the current to flow to the light bulb, in which a heated filament produces light; or I might argue that students who sit in the front of the classroom are more likely to pay attention and less likely to be distracted by posts on social media than those who sit farther back, so that the students in front learn more and thereby perform better on tests, leading to higher grades. And I might further be able to connect my explanations to authorities who have written about how electric currents work or how focusing improves learning. All of this is fairly straightforward. All causal arguments need such rationales.

Nonspuriousness

Nonspuriousness: a fancy word, but an important one. An apparently causal relationship—one that meets the standards of precedence, patterned variation, and rationale—still might be invalid because that relationship is spurious,: that is, caused by some third factor.

Here, it may help to begin with a silly example. Suppose that, after observing the switch-light pattern—up, on; down, off—I announce that flicking the switch down is causing the light to turn off, and vice versa. But Tonya responds, "No, the light is controlled by invisible leprechauns who mischievously choose to turn the light on or off whenever you flick the switch. The real cause of the light going on is the leprechauns' magical powers!"

As I say, this is a ridiculous objection, one we are likely to reject out of hand—but why? Well, first of all, we have a solid rationale, elaborate theories of electricity and how it works, theories that have been tested in countless experiments, so we have a great deal of confidence in our rationale. Moreover, we don't have any evidence that leprechauns exist. "But," Tonya responds, "that's because leprechauns' magical powers allow them to avoid being detected."

Can we *absolutely* prove that leprechauns don't cause the lights to go on and off? Well, no. But there is a very old philosophical principle—often called Occam's razor—that when we have two explanations (in this case, the electrical-circuit explanation and the electrical-circuit-plus-leprechauns explanation) that predict equally well, we should favor the simpler explanation. That is, if we can adequately explain the lights going on and off without incorporating leprechauns in our explanation, we should lose the leprechauns.

Occam's razor allows us to dismiss explanations that invoke various unobservable causes (such as leprechauns). But charges of spuriousness—that some other cause is at work—can take serious forms. Suppose we want to argue that smoking causes lung cancer. Ted might object: smokers, he observes, tend to drink more alcohol than nonsmokers; perhaps it is alcohol that causes lung cancer, or perhaps it is the combination of tobacco plus alcohol. Ted's critique may seem more plausible than invoking leprechauns, and it cannot be dismissed out of hand. We will need to look for more evidence, perhaps by comparing lung cancer rates among various groups:

nonsmokers, smokers who don't drink, drinkers who don't smoke, and smokers who drink. And suppose our new evidence shows that smoking does seem to increase the risk of lung cancer, even after we take drinking into account. "Okay," Ted might say, "but smokers also drink more coffee than nonsmokers"—a critique that sets up a new round of tests.

When can we absolutely, positively declare that a relationship is nonspurious? That is, when can we say we have identified the cause of some effect, and there is no other possible explanation? The answer may seem a little disturbing: never. It is always possible for a critic to argue that some other factor may explain the relationship between what we think is the cause and what we consider the effect of that cause. Now, to be sure, we may compile vast amounts of evidence consistent with our explanation, such as the thousands of studies supporting the conclusion that smoking damages human health—so much evidence that it seems very unlikely that tobacco isn't dangerous and we have great confidence in declaring that it is harmful. And yet, we can never completely exclude the possibility that this well-documented relationship might be spurious.

This is why critical thinking is so important. Every explanation can be challenged. But those challenges can themselves be evaluated. One cannot simply announce that all scientific knowledge must be wrong, that the world is in fact being run by leprechauns. In discussions among scientists, challenges must be subject to the same sorts of evaluations as the arguments being challenged. That is, we expect both those offering explanations and those challenging them to support their claims with evidence, and all that evidence must be weighed and judged. We must hold both explanations and challenges to the same high standards.

Judging Social Scientific Claims

Judging scientific reasoning—and that includes the social sciences—revolves around assessing evidence. Claims must be supported by presenting evidence consistent with what is being claimed, and critics must be able to evaluate that evidence.

Because evidence is central to science, scientists are under an obligation to be honest in reporting their evidence. They are expected to find the best possible evidence, to explain clearly how they went about assembling and analyzing that evidence, and to report their findings in a thorough and accurate manner. It is considered scandalous when scientists are found to have behaved dishonestly, and being implicated in a single scandal can destroy an individual's entire scientific reputation.[5]

Such scandals aside, debates often arise around the quality and interpretation of evidence. Any one study is inevitably flawed—there is no such thing as perfection—and critics can always raise legitimate questions about its evidence. For instance, they can argue that the manner in which the researcher gathered evidence or the methods chosen to analyze that evidence may have affected the results. A single research report is unlikely to be taken as the last word on anything, which is why the news media's tendency to hype dramatic new research "breakthroughs" often fosters the spread of bad information. Because every study has limitations that might have affected its results—and researchers—like everyone else—may find it difficult to think critically about what might be wrong with their research. Therefore, other researchers, rather than simply accepting the original claims, may be inspired to conduct their own studies: either to replicate the first study to see whether following the reported procedures a second time produces the same findings, or to use slightly different procedures to see whether the original techniques may have shaped the findings. The outcome of this work can help reveal whether the patterned variation is spurious.

Debating evidence is the central focus of most critical thinking about research in the social sciences. If this seems surprising, it shouldn't. This chapter has used arguments that may seem straightforward. I chose the example of leprechauns causing lights to go on and off precisely because it is ridiculous. And while it might seem reasonable that sitting near the front of the classroom leads to higher grades, there are no doubt many, many reasons why students get the grades they do—how much and how well they studied, were they healthy or sick when they took their tests, and on and on. The claims that smoking causes disease is an argument that is now very familiar, but it has a long history. The tobacco industry waged a decades-long campaign to challenge researchers' claims that smoking was dangerous; it mounted dozens of arguments that the apparent link between smoking and disease was a spurious relationship, that the true culprit might be alcohol or coffee or . . . you get the idea. Eventually, a vast research literature consisting of thousands of studies using different research designs established an edifice of evidence that has convinced most people that smoking is indeed risky.[6]

All scientific knowledge, then, rests on a foundation of evidence. The bigger and better the foundation, the more confidence we have in what we know. Given the mountain of assembled evidence, very few people today doubt that smoking is harmful. Still, it is always possible that a relationship generally considered causal is in fact spurious. What we think we know today may be challenged if compelling new evidence emerges tomorrow. And most questions that we care about—what causes disease, for example, or what leads to better grades—are likely to have complicated answers, so that evaluating the evidence can become a very elaborate process.

This is why most undergraduate and graduate programs in the social sciences feature required courses in statistics and methodology. While on the surface these topics may seem less interesting than more substantive subjects, they provide essential lessons for social scientists who need to understand how to conduct research so as to produce the most convincing evidence possible. Indeed, understanding best practices can give all students—not just those who plan to become researchers—the tools needed to assess reports about research results. Everyone needs to understand the pitfalls of doing research in ways that are likely to distort one's findings, because throughout our lives we will encounter claims about what researchers have found, and being an informed citizen requires being able to think critically about those reports.

The Importance of Evidence

Social science involves a search for knowledge that is supported by the best available evidence. This evidence is never perfect; it is always subject to critical evaluation. Science advances not through pronouncements about what is true, but by dialogues between those making claims and critics seeking to weigh the strength of evidence.

Evidence is central to all the social sciences, but because the various disciplines examine somewhat different topics and ask distinctive questions, the specific challenges for critical thinking vary among the social sciences.. So let's turn our attention from the social sciences in general and focus on sociology.

Critical Thinking Takeaways

- Causal explanations are judged by the standards of precedence, patterned variation, rationale, and nonspuriousness. It is never possible to establish that a relationship absolutely is not spurious.
- Most critical thinking in the social sciences involves judging the quality of evidence.

5 *Authority and Social Science Arguments*

We are all products of our schooling. From childhood, we have been taught to treat our lessons as authoritative. When we memorized the multiplication table, we were told that 3 × 3 = 9—that this was a truth that should not, could not, be questioned. (To be sure, this claim is supported by evidence: for instance, if you take three groups of three pennies and add them all up, you'll find you have nine.)

Of course, we also learned that not all lessons were that cut-and-dried, that there are gradations in how much authority we ought to grant to what we were learning. Around third grade, most of us probably had a social studies unit on distinguishing facts and opinions, in which we learned that while facts are indisputably, really true, opinions are claims about matters where people may disagree, even if they strongly believe that what they think is true. Thus, while we all should agree that 3 × 3 = 9 is a fact, we should also acknowledge that people have differing opinions about who is the best superhero.

By the time we reach high school, we are encouraged to think more subtly, to understand that opinions can be supported by more or less evidence. This means that while there can be different interpretations about, say, the causes of particular historical events or how to interpret symbolism in different works of literature, although some of these claims may be considered more convincing than others.

In other words, we can envision authoritativeness as a continuum, with solid ($3 \times 3 = 9$) facts at one end, and completely unsupported opinions ("I don't know why I think Superman is the best superhero, I just do") at the other. Thus, education encourages us to recognize and defer to authority, even as it teaches us that not all claims are equally authoritative, that we can and should evaluate the evidence for different claims.

Deference to authority is most pronounced for claims in the natural sciences and far weaker for those in the humanities. That is, when physicists and chemists assure me that a run-of-the-mill oxygen atom has eight electrons, I (and they) treat this as a straightforward fact, because I assume (and I figure they must know) that this claim is supported by a vast edifice of research. I don't know (mainly because I can't demonstrate it myself) whether this knowledge is as certain as $3 \times 3 = 9$, but it must be close. On the other hand, when a literature professor tells me that a particular reading of *Hamlet* is *the* correct one, I may suspect that this is just one of a host of competing interpretations, each with its own advocates (and that there are doubtless graduate students out there in English departments beavering away on other interpretations as we speak).

The authority of the social sciences lies on the continuum of authority somewhere between that of the typically regarded-as-factual natural sciences and that of the seemingly opinion-based humanities. As we noted in chapter 4, the social sciences' authority comes from their ability to supply evidence to support their claims. Such evidence is subject to critiques, and may be judged to be relatively strong or relatively weak as a result.

Challenges for Social Science

Sociology is, of course, one of the social sciences. Each of the social sciences takes a somewhat different approach—adopts a different perspective—for understanding human behavior. Thus, economics argues that people seek to achieve their goals by making calculated choices, while psychology aims to explain the behavior of individual organisms (be they rats or people) [Sociology's central insight is that people affect one another, and its goal is to explore the ways those social effects occur and the patterns they reveal.]

Obviously, there are points at which social science disciplines overlap: social psychology, for example—how social influences shape individual behavior—is of interest to both psychologists and sociologists; similarly, there are sociologists who adopt economic models to study how calculated decisions—rational choices—shape social life, just as some economists study how social arrangements influence people's decision-making. But each of the social sciences adopts a somewhat distinctive perspective for understanding people's behavior, emphasizing different aspects of people's lives.

None of the social sciences offers a comprehensive understanding of humanity; all have limitations. Economics—probably the most prestigious social science (and hang on: we'll get to sociology in a moment)—devises sophisticated models, but those models have obvious shortcomings when trying to predict people's actual economic behavior. In theory, markets should reflect the rational calculations of their participants, but in reality markets get caught up in "irrational exuberance," in which prices rise only to collapse—the familiar boom-and-bust cycle.[1] *Behavioral economics* has emerged as a specialty among economists who seek to understand why people's behavior in the real world often falls short of the rationality that economics assumes to exist.

In seeking to understand people's actions, behavioral economists turn to psychological explanations. They conduct experiments in which the subjects are asked to make decisions under varying conditions; the results reveal that many people make choices that are not—by economists' standards—perfectly rational. For instance, they may exhibit a strong preference among a set of choices that economic theory states should be considered equally beneficial, or they may even prefer a less beneficial outcome under some circumstances. Behavioral economists then explain these patterns as the results of psychological processes, such as *anchoring* (i.e., being excessively influenced by some initial piece of information) or *information avoidance* (choosing not to obtain readily available information). Since economic models usually assume that people have the information they need to make rational choices, both anchoring and information avoidance point to reasons why real-world individuals—and markets—may not behave as predicted. Economists can then invoke these processes to explain why markets display irrational exuberance or other patterns that contradict the predictions of economic models.

This line of reasoning has its challenges. Behavioral economists have identified a long list of psychological processes that sometimes describe contradictory tendencies. In a particular situation, for instance, if individuals seem reluctant to take action, economists may apply the label *status quo bias,* whereas people who seem eager to act are designated as having an *action bias.* Given a sufficiently long list of these patterns, it becomes possible to explain—after the fact—pretty much anything people do. Of course, assigning a name to a behavior is very different from being able to predict which patterns will appear in set circumstances: economists will likely never be able to say when and how people will fail to behave as economic models predict. Another challenge is that trying to explain the behavior of large institutions—such as a suddenly collapsing stock market—by invoking individual psychological processes ignores the surrounding context of social life.

The space between individuals with their idiosyncratic psychologies, on the one hand, and great, abstract institutions such as the stock market, on the other, is sociology's turf. A market is not composed of unconnected individuals, but rather of people who are nestled into webs of social relationships. People are linked to families and friends, and to people with whom they work, worship, and play. Sociologists speak of these as *social worlds,* networks of people who share activities and often perspectives on their lives. Sociological interpretations focus less on cognitive processes occurring within individuals' brains—anchoring, action bias, and so forth—and more on the effects individuals have on one another's behavior. For sociologists, critical thinking usually involves unpacking those social influences.

The Case of Sociology

Like economists and psychologists, sociologists tend to act as though their discipline's claims are authoritative. This is of course putting on a bold front. As we have already noted, most people think the authority of the social sciences stands somewhere between that of the natural sciences and that of the humanities. But even within the social sciences, many question sociologists' authority.

Sociology's public reputation is mixed. Most often, its critics charge that sociology is basically just common sense, that it adds little to what everyone already knows. Further, they complain that sociologists try to disguise the obviousness of their observations by cloaking them in dense, nearly incomprehensible jargon. And there is the additional complaint that sociology has a liberal political bias, that its approach is more ideological than scientific.[2] These have been common criticisms for decades.

Nonetheless, sociology has a reasonably well-established place in academia This reflects the fact that sociology has been the source of many useful ideas that have shaped modern thought, including such concepts as charisma, moral panic, role model, significant other, status symbol, and subculture.[3] Sociological ideas get picked up because lots of people find them to be useful ways of thinking about the world. Similarly, sociologists have been instrumental in pioneering methods for studying social life, such as survey research. Not only does sociologists' terminology creep into popular culture, but their theoretical approaches and methodologies have shaped thinking in other disciplines, including criminology, demography, law, management, marketing, medicine, political science, and social work. In fact, some of these disciplines originated in sociology departments before splitting off to form their own academic units.

Sociology has been influential, despite being frequently dismissed as unimportant or irrelevant. Even after serious attacks, the discipline has been able to bounce back. In the 1990s, for example, Washington University in St. Louis decided to close its sociology department, suggesting to some that the discipline was in serious trouble. The reports of sociology's imminent death turned out to be greatly exaggerated, however—as signaled by Washington University's reestablishment of its sociology department in 2015.

Thinking about Sociology and Critical Thinking

Still, sociologists' authority seems more precarious than that of, say, economists. And this situation underpins the argument in the rest of this book. I want to argue that critical thinking is especially important for sociologists, not least because the discipline is so often challenged. What sociologists have to say has always attracted criticism, and not just from outsiders. As we will see, there has been a good deal of bickering among sociologists as well.

Like physicists, philosophers, and other academics, sociologists claim authority for what they say. Sociologists have, after all, received specialized training in sociological theory and methodology, which should qualify them to conduct and interpret research. Physicists, philosophers, and other academics make analogous claims for their own authority.

But having such credentials does not mean that sociologists' claims cannot or should not be subjected to critical evaluation. Just as it is possible to think critically about the claims of economists and psychologists, so can we assess what sociologists have to say. As we have already established, critical thinking is an appropriate response to any and all claims, regardless of the credentials of the people who make them. And as always, it is most important—and most difficult—to think critically about our own ideas.

But how should we approach critical thinking about sociology? This book begins by applying a sociological perspective to sociology as a discipline, viewing sociology itself as a social world and trying to understand how that world is organized and how its members think about what they are doing.[4] The remaining chapters examine how sociologists' social world shapes what they do and explore the kinds of questions critics might ask about what sociologists have to say.

While this book's focus will remain on sociology, sociology is not unique. Most of the points we will explore are relevant to the other social sciences, such as anthropology, economics, and political science. Each of these disciplines has and is shaped by its own social world, and many of the problems that challenge sociologists are common to the other social sciences.

Sociologists are interested in a variety of research questions; they adopt different techniques to try to answer those questions, and they do not always agree. You need to understand that while I am a sociologist, I am speaking for myself, and I realize that other sociologists might disagree with what I have to say on various points. I am trying to spell out what I do when I try to think critically about sociology, and why I think the questions that I ask are worthwhile. I cannot claim that I have special authority—while I tried to think critically about what I was saying when I wrote this book, I realize that others might reject some of my claims, and they would undoubtedly want to make arguments of their own. But we have to start somewhere. So let's begin by examining the social world of sociology.

Critical Thinking Takeaway

- Claims of authority should be critically evaluated.

6 *Sociology as a Social World*

Although some people who earn Ph.D. degrees in sociology go on to work for government agencies, public opinion polling firms, and so on, most sociologists teach in colleges or universities. These range from two-year community colleges where faculty may teach five or more courses per term, to Ph.D.-granting departments in research universities where faculty typically teach two classes a term. In general, institutions with heavier teaching loads do not expect faculty members to do much research; the expectation that professors should be active researchers rises as the teaching load falls.

Research is usually understood to lead to publication. The expression "publish or perish" has been around for decades—a warning to new professors that it may be impossible to receive tenure and promotion without publishing. This usually involves having one's articles appear in professional journals. Publication is treated as evidence that an individual is making significant contributions to their discipline. And sociology offers many paths to publishing.

Camps

Thus far, we have been treating sociology as a single discipline united by an interest in the ways people affect one another. While sociologists share this basic approach, they may disagree about the best way to think about particular topics. Imagine several sociologists thinking about studying what goes on in a restaurant. The first sociologist, let's call her Anna, might approach the restaurant as a workplace, looking at the division of labor among the restaurant's employees, and how the cooks in the kitchen and the servers who deal with customers manage their jobs. In contrast, Bill might be a sociologist of food, interested in the processes by which food is produced and consumed, as well as in the meanings that food has for the various people involved in those processes. Carol might examine the role gender plays in shaping interactions among the restaurant staff and their customers, while Dwayne might concentrate on the impact of race and ethnicity, and Ellen might argue that it is most helpful to think about the ways gender and race intersect. Frank, a sociologist of deviance, might look at how norms are violated—and we could easily go on. There are many ways to think sociologically, and that's a good thing. Different sociologists can view even an apparently mundane setting like a restaurant from different angles, and each will notice slightly different things.

All of these sociologists share the underlying assumption that people affect one another, although each is interested in different effects. Most sociologists specialize in two or three topics: there are sociologists of work, and of gender, food, religion, education, race and ethnicity, sports, and deviance. Name something that involves humans, there's probably a sociologist studying it. One obvious way to think about the organization of sociology as a discipline is in terms of these various substantive specialties. After all, once past the introductory class, virtually all sociology courses focus on specialized topics, and often the instructor specializes in that subject.

But there are other ways to carve up the discipline. Many sociologists see themselves as generally aligned with a particular theoretical school or approach, such as symbolic interactionism, conflict theory, or rational-choice theory. And most sociologists favor particular methods when conducting research, the most basic distinction being between quantitative sociologists (who use statistics to analyze numeric data) and qualitative sociologists (who tend to collect data through observations or interviews); and each of those general approaches can be subdivided into more specific methodologies, such as survey research.

So, if we ask sociologists "What sort of sociologist are you?", their responses may indicate interests in specific substantive topics, as well as preferences for particular theoretical and methodological approaches.

We can think of sociology as composed of various schools of thought—let's call them camps—based on these substantive interests, theoretical orientations, and methodological preferences. As sociology has grown, it has become impossible for an individual to keep track of everything going on in the discipline. The best most people can do is try to stay more or less current with what's going on in the couple of camps that interest them most.

Camps give sociology much of its structure. Sociologists report on their research through presentations at professional conferences or by publishing in academic journals and books. When sociology emerged as a discipline, the American Sociological Society (founded in 1905 and later renamed an Association—so it is now the ASA) and regional bodies such as the Southern Sociological Society (founded in 1935) might meet in a single room, so that someone attending a conference could hear all of the papers being presented, but as the discipline expanded multiple sessions began being conducted at the same time in different rooms. These days, the largest professional association—the ASA—runs dozens of simultaneous sessions, some of which are designated as roundtable sessions that are further subdivided into dozens of tables at each of which people sit listening to presentations, each organized around a specific topic or theme, so that people must choose to attend the presentations that most interest them. This has had the effect of dividing the discipline as a whole, even as it brings together people who belong to the same camps. Similarly, the larger associations now contain specialized units organized around different camps. Thus, the ASA has more than fifty formal sections for those interested in particular substantive topics (e.g., environmental sociology, sociology of culture), theories (Marxist sociology, rationality and society), or methodologies (comparative historical sociology, methodology).

Parallel developments have shaped publishing. A 1968 article attempted to list every American sociology journal: at that time there were sixteen journals publishing articles, of which nine— more than half—were of a general nature, at least theoretically open to publishing contributions on all sociological topics.[1] Today, there are well over a hundred sociology journals, and all but about ten focus on specialized topics, with names such as *Sociology of Sport Journal, Gender and Society,* or *City & Community.* Similarly, most scholarly book publishers tend to specialize in books about particular subjects or that adopt distinctive approaches.

In short, most sociological camps have their own associations (or at least subdivisions within larger organizations), their own journals, and even their own publishers—venues where members can present or publish their work. The venues have gatekeepers— conference organizers, editors at journals and publishing houses—

who sift through submitted work and choose which research is worthy of dissemination. Camp members learn to follow what's happening in the venues that interest them.

All this means that two colleagues in adjacent offices in a university's sociology department are quite likely to belong to different camps: they probably teach courses on different topics and read different books and journals. In effect, they have less in common with each other than with their fellow camp members who work on other campuses nationwide, even worldwide.

There is a sense in which different camps function as rivals. Each camp's members share ideas, agreeing that this topic, theory, or method is especially interesting or useful. They tend to attend the same meetings, and read and publish in the same journals. They affirm the value of their own approach to one another, and they may view what's happening in other camps as uninteresting or even wrongheaded. In particular, camps centered around particular theoretical orientations or methodological approaches tend to be especially impatient with rival schools of thought.[2] This leads to a tendency for people to talk mostly to those who share their assumptions, while spending less time following, let alone debating, those in other camps. Camps often favor particular terminology, so they have difficulty understanding—and may talk past—one another. It is much easier and more comfortable to devote time and attention to others who share your perspective, rather than confront those who challenge your ideas.

Of course, a camp's gatekeepers usually identify firmly with that camp. This means that when you submit a manuscript to a journal read by the members of your camp, both the journal's editor and the peer reviewers who evaluate it are usually also camp members. Peer reviewers evaluate submissions for journals: their reactions may vary from declaring the paper to be perfect as it is (a rare occurrence), to offering suggestions for improvement, to arguing that it is so badly flawed that the editor should refuse to publish it. In theory, the identity of the author(s) is unknown to the reviewers, and the reviewers are not identified to the authors (although it is sometimes possible to guess who's who).

Peer review is seen as an important safeguard for the publishing process, intended to help catch and correct errors before they can be published. At the same time, journals that exist to publish works by and for members of an intellectual camp usually assign reviewers who are members of the camp. After all, it seems unfair to send the manuscript to reviewers outside the camp (who may have more difficulty understanding—and are more likely to be critical of—the work). But this raises a problem: reviewers who likely share the author's assumptions may have more difficulty thinking critically about the paper's contents—its premise, its methods, its conclusions. Staying within the camp minimizes conflict by ensuring that submissions are evaluated by sympathetic reviewers and editors. Once accepted, these papers will appear in the pages of journals where the readers also tend to belong to the camp.

Camps offer protected enclaves, where sociologists who share substantive interests and theoretical and methodological preferences can communicate with one another, while minimizing the risks of having to defend their ideas from others who do not share their assumptions. But if the most difficult—and the most important—forms of critical thinking involve critiquing one's own ideas, then exposing our work primarily to those most likely to agree with us is not the best way to get critical feedback.

Envy

Sociologists occupy a modest place in the academic pecking order. Within universities, they are seen as neither so rigorous as "real scientists" like physicists and chemists, nor as intellectually sophisticated as philosophers and others in the humanities who pursue "truth and beauty." As we noted in chapter 5, the rap against sociologists is that they disguise commonsense findings with incomprehensible jargon. Sociologists can be sensitive to and defensive about these critiques. They may envy others who seem better regarded, and seek ways to conduct themselves to silence the critics. This envy most often takes one of three forms.

Physics Envy

Some sociologists prefer to emphasize that theirs is a scientific discipline, that the logic of their research resembles that of physicists or chemists who derive hypotheses and test them using precise methods. Natural scientists are widely admired; they receive Nobel Prizes. In contrast, people tend to be a little suspicious of sociology; they wonder whether it isn't really just common sense. After all, there's no Nobel Prize for sociology.

One response to this disrespect is for sociologists to focus intently on methodology, devising complicated tests of hypotheses and analyzing the results using sophisticated statistical techniques. Sociology's premier journals spotlight this sort of research. As I write this, the newest issue of the *American Sociological Review* contains tables showing results of "stochastic actor-oriented models for the co-evolution of networks and behavior," logistic regression, residual balancing, hierarchical growth-curve models, and so on. Only a tiny fraction of people can read and fully understand such tables. Isn't that proof that sociology can be just as sophisticated as physics?

Herein lies danger. The justification for using sophisticated statistics is that they can allow analysts to unpack complex information. But these techniques usually require a lot of high-quality data. In most cases, for statistical tests to be meaningful, those data need to be representative—that is, they don't exclude particular sorts of cases. The problem is that a collection of social data will almost certainly be biased in some way. For instance, census data might seem to be a good source of information, because the census theoretically counts everyone. But in practice, we know that the census misses about 1 or 2 percent of the population, and the people who are missed tend to be different—poorer, more likely to be non-white—than those who are counted. One might argue that, for most purposes, a census that counts 98 or 99 percent of the population ought to provide pretty good data; however, because they aren't truly representative, such data are not good enough. Typically, sociologists suffering from physics envy gloss over this problem: they briefly acknowledge that maybe their data aren't perfect, but then go on to reason that there sure is a lot of it, so if we just assume that the data are pretty good, then we can use high-powered statistics.

The other problem with having lots of data is that it makes it easier to have "statistically significant" results. Because scholarly journals rarely publish articles that don't report statistically significant findings, researchers tend to view achieving statistical significance as a research goal. But, while "statistically significant" sounds as though it must be important, that's not what the term means. Statistical significance basically measures the likelihood that a researcher's observation of a sample is due to mere chance, rather than to a pattern that actually exists in a population. It has nothing to do with whether a finding is important. If a researcher has enough data, even very small differences—differences that might not be apparent to people in the course of living their lives—can achieve statistical significance. Suppose your risk of contracting some terrible but rare disease is 1 in 10,000, and further suppose that smoking doubles that risk, so that you now have 2 chances in 10,000 of getting sick. That might be a statistically significant finding, but the effect is so small you aren't likely to notice it. When reading research, it is always important to ask whether the effects being reported are large enough to be noticed in people's real-world, everyday lives.

The term "physics envy" is an exaggeration, of course; I don't mean to suggest that quantitative sociologists literally seethe because they don't receive the same respect as natural scientists. But sophisticated statistics encourage the sociologists who understand them to find ways to apply them. Philosophers speak of the Law of the Instrument: "Give a small boy a hammer, and he'll find things to pound." Statistics offer a whole tool bench of hammers, and the temptation to start swinging them can distort sociologists' thinking.

Philosophy Envy

While physics envy tempts some sociologists to overvalue their methods, other sociologists devalue methodology—especially elaborate research designs and sophisticated statistics—in favor of theory. They are drawn to theoretical abstraction, to thinking "big thoughts." They suffer from what we might call philosophy envy.

These are the folks who are responsible for much of sociology's reputation for jargon and bad writing. They love to borrow lingo from big-time philosophers—terms like *ontology, epistemology,* and *hermeneutics.* They are fascinated by abstractions, and they enjoy raising what they see as deep issues, such as how can we know anything? When they do direct their attention to the social world, they put great stock is defining terms and inventing new words to denote the unique insights they are developing. If it is difficult to make sense of their writing, then they must be doing something pretty impressive. And if someone complains that what they write is hard to follow, that merely shows that the critic doesn't understand sophisticated reasoning.

Those suffering from philosophy envy can be fabulous critical thinkers—when they are criticizing others.[3] They level devastating critiques about the unwarranted assumptions that form the foundations for others' work. As we might expect, they can be hard on the quantitative sociologists with their fixation on methodology, but they often direct their most scathing critiques at those adopting rival theoretical perspectives. So long as they can remain tucked within the fortress of their own abstractions, they can fend off criticism, but problems tend to arise when they try to venture out to actually study social behavior. At that point, they find themselves compromising, making the same sorts of assumptions that they attack others for making.

Although they might seem to be opposites, physics envy and philosophy envy both lead to the same problem: their proponents find it easy to lose track of the social patterns that are the very stuff of sociology. Both forms of envy lead to sociologists becoming so infatuated with *what* they're doing that they sometimes forget *why* they're doing it. While in the end they may prove that they can do something very complicated, few are interested in the result.

Protest Envy

A third temptation attracts some sociologists: social activism. Many intellectuals are sensitive to criticism that they live in ivory towers, divorced from the real world. This can be particularly problematic for people who entered sociology because they were concerned about and wanted to help address social problems. Some sociologists, proudly labeling themselves *scholar-activists,* declare that their scholarship is intended to advance social justice. These sociologists also suffer from a form of envy—of in-the-streets activists. Because the vast majority of sociologists think of themselves as politically liberal, progressive, or radical, the activists they envy are almost always on the left.[4]

Obviously, there is nothing wrong with sociologists having political opinions, any more than with their having religious beliefs or musical tastes.[5] But problems can arise when their opinions shape the results of their research. Researchers make all sorts of choices—they choose what they'll study, how they'll go about studying it, and how they'll interpret their results. Those choices inevitably affect their research findings. This is why sociologists need to be careful to detail their choices—to spell out their methods, so that their readers can evaluate how their choices may have affected the results of the research. They need to be sure their political views do not lead them to skew the reported results, or cause them to overlook, dismiss, or reject the findings of sociologists who happen to have different views.

Ultimately, social scientific critiques should center on the evaluation of evidence. It is not appropriate to ignore evidence simply because we disagree with the person who collected it—that would be a form of ad hominem reasoning. It may be possible to criticize the *choices* made that produced that evidence—and those choices may indeed have been shaped by that person's political beliefs—but it is those choices' effects on the research results that should be the focus of criticism, not the underlying beliefs themselves.

These three varieties of envy—physics envy, philosophy envy, and protest envy—can all lead sociologists astray, causing them to produce evidence that is less useful. In each case, there is a temptation to give priority to an abstraction—methodological rigor, theoretical elegance, or ideological correctness—rather than trying to understand the real workings of social life. The effort to impress others comes at the cost of sociological insight.

Sociology's Subdivisions

This chapter has argued that, while sociology has some influence within academia, its position is tenuous. Sociologists are defensive about this. Partly for this reason, and partly as a response to the discipline's growth, they have organized into camps—clusters of people who share particular approaches to sociology. This fragmentation helps explain why critics worry that sociology lacks a central *core*—a basic framework that is shared by all the discipline's members.[6] We will explore some consequences of this in later chapters.

Critical Thinking Takeaways

- As a discipline, sociology is organized into intellectual camps centered on particular substantive topics, methodologies, or theories.
- Sociologists can lose sight of sociology's goal of understanding how people affect one another, and focus instead on methodological rigor, theoretical sophistication, or social activism.

7 *Orientations*

Sociologists realize that people view the world in different ways. In part, this variation reflects one's position in society; we recognize that people of different ages, genders, educations, ethnicities, occupations, religions, or social classes are likely to have had different experiences, to have been socialized into somewhat different cultures, and to have different interests, all of which may shape their perspectives on their own lives and on the wider society. Much of what sociologists do involves comparing the attitudes or behaviors of people who occupy different social positions.

Being a sociologist is itself a social position with its own point of view. Sociologists acquire a sociological perspective that leads them to be attuned to the ways people affect one another, and as we have seen, many sociologists belong to camps that highlight particular theoretical, methodological, or substantive matters. Like everyone else, sociologists may be shaped by their various identities—as sociologists (which causes them to approach the world differently than, say economists, psychologists, or historians) and as members of particular camps; and no doubt by their belonging to particular classes, genders, ethnicities, and so on.

In addition, sociologists have different *orientations*, that can shape how they understand the world. We can think of these as different temperaments that can underpin sociologists' arguments and, in turn affect how they approach critical thinking. This chapter will discuss some dimensions along which sociologists' orientations vary.

Optimism and Pessimism

Although we tend to think of optimism and pessimism as psychological traits, these are also orientations that can steer sociologists' interpretations of the world.

Optimism

Optimists have upbeat expectations that, in general, things tend to improve. Within sociology, optimism is linked to the idea of progress. Some early sociologists—influenced by the emergence of the theory of evolution—suggested that human history could be viewed as a sort of social evolution, in which earlier, simpler forms of society such as hunters and gatherers evolved into more complicated forms such as the industrial societies of their own time. Because sociology arose in response to the industrial revolution, many of the most influential early sociological theorists viewed social change in terms of emerging societal types, such as Emile Durkheim's mechanical and organic solidarity or Ferdinand Tönnies's *Gemeinschaft* and *Gesellschaft*. Karl Marx's vision of history as marching inevitably toward a communist utopia is another expression of evolutionary progress. Early sociology, then, seemed relatively optimistic.

Claims for progress tend to involve measures of material well-being. Throughout most of human history, average life expectancy at birth was roughly thirty years, largely because about half of children died before their sixth birthday; today, of course, life expectancies are decades higher. Surely, optimists argue, this represents progress. Similarly, measures of literacy and nutrition show improvements. Contemporary theorists argue that this reflects the dramatic growth and spread of scientific knowledge.[1] Optimists, in short, recognize the possibility of improvement. Although they acknowledge that things can get worse, they believe that humans have the ability to understand how the world works and use that knowledge to improve things.

Critics identify several problems with optimism as an orientation. There is no guarantee that things must improve, they argue, nor that the benefits of progress will be equally available to all; there is also the possibility that apparent advances will prove temporary, that even what seem like settled accomplishments can disappear following a societal collapse.[2] In spite of all the evidence for progress in recent centuries, contemporary sociologists seem temperamentally more inclined toward pessimism.

Pessimism

The pessimist's concern is that things are getting—and are likely to continue to get—worse. Often, this impression is coupled with a view of history that emphasizes decline.[3] The critique is familiar: in the good old days, children respected their parents and listened to their teachers, adults obeyed the law and had strong religious faith, everyone knew their place and took pride in their work, and society functioned smoothly. But things have slipped badly, and we can only imagine how much worse things are going to become.

Tales of decline are often told by political conservatives suspicious of change, which might seem to make sociologists unlikely to adopt this viewpoint. But there is a form of pessimism popular among liberals as well (which, as we have noted, includes most sociologists), who point to the obstacles that seem to stand unmoving in the face of needed change. In their view, racism, sexism, and the class system threaten to block or undo all progress.

Selective evidence provides support for pessimism. "Today's schools are failing," cries Pete the Pessimist. "But," you respond, "more people are staying in school longer than ever before." "Maybe so," says Pete, "but they aren't learning the way students did in my day. Why, just yesterday at the store the cashier had trouble making change." This anecdote invites us to believe that, back in the day, everyone always made the correct change.

Even really big improvements can be dismissed. Tell Pete that people today have the longest life expectancy in history, and he'll grumble, "But people used to be happier." No, Pete doesn't have a happy-ometer that allows him to measure mood swings over time; he is just sure that people used to be happier before things started getting worse.

Pessimism often takes the form of nostalgia, in which people recall a rosy past. Sociologists' nostalgia often centers around the loss of community. In the good old days, they insist, people lived in close-knit towns and neighborhoods where people knew one another and everyone had a sense of belonging. Modern societies, in contrast, are more anonymous, more—to use a favorite sociological term—anomic. Several of sociology's all-time bestsellers have titles that tap into this theme: *The Lonely Crowd, The Pursuit of Loneliness, Bowling Alone.* In this view, loneliness and the loss of community are problems of modern life.

There are a couple of problems with this vision. The first is that it ignores the conditions of life in those premodern communities—places where, remember, half of newborns died before they turned six and where women were expected to be subservient. Certainly the world has changed, but, regardless of the pessimists' nattering, it is obvious that many, if not most, of these changes have been for the better.

Pessimism, like optimism, is a poor guide for thinking about social change. Whether things have improved or gotten worse is something sociologists might try to measure. This would require devising some standards for assessing the goodness-of-things, and others would be free to critique those standards and the way the measurements were carried out. We might find that some things have improved, while others have declined. Presuming—as both optimists and pessimists tend to do—that there is one dominant pattern is probably a mistake.

Team Culture and Team Structure

Culture and social structure are ideas central to sociologists' thinking. *Culture* basically refers to everything that people know—to the language they use to classify the world and the meanings they assign to those classifications. Culture is the central concept in anthropology, because early anthropologists traveled to distant places and recorded how the people living there understood their worlds. Those people had different languages, different customs, and different beliefs, so it was easy to identify the distinctive features of those cultures, which contrasted so sharply from how the anthropologists understood their own ordinary, everyday world.

It is more challenging to recognize our own culture; being immersed in it, we simply assume that our understanding of the world is correct, normal, sensible. This is why sociology relies on comparisons, which reveal that people who occupy different places in society often see things differently. This discovery delivers a little jolt—the realization that our taken-for-granted viewpoint is not shared by everyone, that our culture is just one among many.

An additional step is needed here: an acknowledgment that just as we consider our culture or viewpoint to be right and normal, so, too, do people in other cultures take it for granted that their own culture is right and normal. All peoples—across time and space— are immersed in their cultures.

Social structure refers to the ways in which social life is organized. Every society that seeks to endure needs males and females, children and adults. Even the smallest groups of hunters and gatherers adhere to social arrangements to divide labor among these different sets of members. Larger societies devise vastly more elaborate social structures based on differences in clan, ethnicity, gender, wealth, status, power, occupation, age, religion, and all the other variables sociologists study.

Culture and social structure reinforce each other in complicated ways. Much of a person's cultural knowledge helps them understand their society's social structure, such that most members learn to take social arrangements for granted, as just the way things are and are supposed to be. At the same time, those social arrangements serve to reproduce culture by, for instance, providing families and schools to teach young people cultural lessons.

At earlier points in human history, most people lived in small, homogeneous communities where people shared a single view of how the world worked. Today, though, relatively few people live in such sheltered circumstances. City life and large, complex societies tend to throw people into contact with lots of different sorts of folks, and media such as television and the Internet expose us to still other kinds of people. However it may disturb us, we must recognize that these people belong to different cultures and subcultures, perhaps eating different foods, wearing distinctive clothes, or behaving in unexpected ways. The need to understand these differences is precisely why sociology exists.

Although culture and social structure affect all people, and are basic concepts in sociology, sociologists often emphasize one and downplay the other. We might think of these as rival teams: Team Culture and Team Structure. One often hears chicken-or-egg debates about which causes the other: is it culture that drives social structure, or social structure that shapes culture? This in turn provokes debates about specific topics within sociology.

Consider poverty. Poverty is one of the oldest concerns for social researchers, the subject of countless studies. So given that we know quite a bit about poverty, it might seem reasonable to ask: What causes poverty? Team Culture and Team Structure promote different answers.

Team Culture

As its name suggests, Team Culture emphasizes culture's role as the principal cause of poverty and many other social conditions. As sociologists use the term, *culture* refers to what people know, including their vocabularies, their norms (that is, what they think of as the rules for behavior), and their values (that is, their ideals). Imagine two subgroups within a society; while both groups probably tell young people that it is important that they do well in school, stay out of trouble with the law, work hard, delay marriage, and avoid early pregnancy, it is also true that one group (which has lots of adults whose lives reflect these goals) consistently emphasizes these lessons, while the other group (whose adults have fallen short of some of these goals) seems less committed to this message. In other words, the two groups have different cultures. The former group may celebrate delaying gratification as a route to success, while the latter may convey a sense of fatalism that it is impossible for young people to do much to improve their lives. We might expect that children raised in the former culture will tend to do better in school than those who have been exposed to less consistent messages.[4]

These days, Team Culture tends to attract political conservatives, who argue that poverty is the result of poor choices (such as dropping out of school or committing delinquent acts) that, in turn, are the product of a flawed culture. They tend to downplay arguments about the role of social structures—class differences and racial discrimination, for example—suggesting instead that the solutions to poverty lie in individuals making better choices.

Team Structure

American society, Team Structure responds, features a lot of inequality—inequality of social class (meaning that some people have vastly higher incomes and greater wealth than others), ethnic inequality (such that nonwhites are less likely to be raised in intact families, have shorter life expectancies, and experience various forms of discrimination), and so on. These structural arrangements make it easier for people who already have advantages to complete school, stay out of trouble, and avoid poverty, while making it more difficult for those with fewer advantages to overcome the obstacles they face.

People who belong to Team Structure tend to be political liberals. They tend to resist explanations that emphasize culture, sometimes using the expression "blaming the victim" (discussed further in chapter 13). In this view, what Team Culture labels poor choices are better understood as creative ways of coping with structural challenges. They would argue that it's hardly surprising that upper-middle-class suburban children do well: after all, they have every advantage. But poor children come from homes where money is tight and security more precarious, and they attend inferior schools that provide fewer routes to opportunities. No wonder some become frustrated or discouraged. Rather than blaming culture for individuals' poor choices, Team Structure insists, we should try to rectify structural problems if we really want to address poverty.

So, Which Is Correct?

You may be thinking that both teams have a point. Poverty is a complicated phenomenon, and it probably doesn't have a single cause—or a single solution. No doubt both culture and social structure play roles in shaping how different individuals behave, which means that we would be well advised to avoid wholeheartedly choosing one team over the other. Insisting that we know the one real cause and refusing outright to consider another point of view oversimplifies the social world. There is no need to declare allegiance to either team. It makes more sense to weigh the evidence to determine when and how culture and social structure have an impact.

Insiders and Outsiders

Inevitably, what we notice about culture and social structure depends on where we're standing. Are we insiders within a particular culture and social structure, so that we tend to take those positions for granted, or are we outsiders, peering into an unfamiliar culture or social structure trying to make sense of things? Anthropologists sometimes refer to these as emic (insider) and etic (outsider) perspectives. It is important to appreciate that both have advantages and disadvantages.

Insiders have a thorough, nuanced understanding of their world, one that outsiders may never fully grasp. However, because they take that world for granted, they may have difficulty recognizing the assumptions they—and that world's other members—make, or to think critically about them. Outsiders, on the other hand, may find it easier to be objective about the world they are examining, but they will always have an imperfect understanding of its subtleties.

In fact, we are all simultaneously insiders and outsiders as we move through the world. Each of us is an individual of a particular age, gender, ethnicity, and height, someone with a unique personal history of experiences. No one else can fully understand where we've been and how we've felt. To some degree, we can consider everyone else an outsider.

This helps explain why there is an autobiographical quality to some sociology. Sociologists who have firsthand experience with an aspect of social life, such as belonging to a particular ethnic group, being a woman, or having worked in a certain occupation, find it easier to recognize why this aspect is sociologically interesting and may be moved to study it. There are countless examples, some going back to American sociology's early decades, such as *The Philadelphia Negro* and other classic works on black America by W. E. B. Du Bois, the great African American sociologist.

No doubt social scientists' findings are shaped to some degree by their insider/outsider status. Such considerations rarely affect discussions about physical scientists. We take it for granted that chemists studying the properties of molecules or astronomers observing the movements of celestial bodies are "outsiders," and we anticipate that the best ways to do chemistry or astronomy involve adopting objective approaches to the subject matter. In contrast, social scientists can get into arguments about whether objectivity is even possible, or desirable.

Outsiders assume that objectivity is as important for social science as is it is for physical science. But insiders argue that such objectivity is impossible, that outsiders can never fully understand the social processes they seek to study. In some cases, they insist that outsiders should not even try to study groups to which they do not belong.

Both of these perspectives have a point, although contemporary sociologists have become more willing to question outsiders' ability to conduct research on some groups, and many recent ethnographies have been written by insiders. It is worth recalling that both insiders and outsiders have advantages and disadvantages, and it is easy to point to fine work written from both perspectives.

Tragedy and Comedy

Given their inclination toward pessimism, it's not surprising that many sociologists view their research in tragic terms, focusing on the frustrations and hardships faced by the people they study. They view their central topic as inequality and the damage it inflicts on individual lives. They tend to focus on social structural arrangements that make people's lives' difficult, and there is an effort to help their readers empathize with the plight of those being studied.

However, some sociologists adopt a more comic—or at least ironic—vision. Much of Erving Goffman's work explored people's seeming obliviousness to the assumptions that underpin their everyday lives. For example, he examined how people, while trying to present themselves in a favorable light to others, in the process manage to convince themselves that they have the qualities they portray. Similarly, he likened how confidence tricksters convince their victims not to complain to the authorities with the ways people help one another deal with the disappointments of everyday life.[5] In other words, putting the best face on things means there will be gaps between people's explanations for their actions and other purposes that they prefer to downplay or conceal. This inconsistency—the gap between what people think (or at least say they think) and what they actually do—can be surprising when it is revealed, all part of the human comedy. Anyone who reads much sociology can point to other examples of work with comic overtones.

In *What's So Funny? The Comic Conception of Culture and Society,* the sociologist Murray S. Davis argues: "Humor laughs at the same phenomena sociology investigates."[6] That is, humor takes on social types and stock situations, patterns in manners, and the violation of expectations, to say nothing of self-deception and hypocrisy. However much some sociologists may sternly insist that there's nothing funny about their research topics, social commentary often takes a comic turn. Think about journalists such as Tom Wolfe and David Brooks who offer amusing—and sociologically informed—analyses with comic overtones.[7] Or consider Parkinson's Law, the idea that work expands to fill the time allotted, or the Peter Principle, which holds that the people in a hierarchy tend to rise to their "level of incompetence"—ideas presented in humorous essays disguised as the work of social scientists that offered pointed critiques of social practices.[8]

The fact that most sociologists favor approaching their topic in tragic terms does not eliminate the possibility of adopting a comic orientation, any more than the current discipline's preferences for pessimism, structural explanations, and the authenticity of insider voices precludes some sociologists from adopting other roads less traveled.

The Importance of Orientations

The topics in this chapter—optimism and pessimism, culture and social structure, insiders and outsiders, and tragedy and comedy—can be viewed as matters of sociological temperament or style. They concern choices sociologists make when deciding how to pursue and present their work. Although some people may be troubled when sociologists adopt some styles, any these styles can be a legitimate choice.

What is the relevance of these orientations to critical thinking? In theory, matters of style might seem to be unimportant when it comes to judging the quality of a sociological argument. But in practice, many sociologists probably find it difficult to evaluate work that adopts a style different from their own. Being aware of orientations can help us place work in its proper context.

Critical Thinking Takeaway

- It may be helpful to consider the orientations that underpin sociological work: Is it optimistic or pessimistic? Does it highlight the role of culture or structure? Does the analyst approach the topic as an insider or an outsider? Is the viewpoint tragic or comic?

8   *Words*

We all depend on language to think. The words we know and the meanings we assign to them shape our thoughts. In this regard, sociologists are just like everyone else; our vocabularies affect our efforts to understand and explain the world. However, because sociologists are trying to explain how and why members of society behave as they do, the words we use need to be chosen with special care. This is inevitably an insider/outsider issue, in that sociologists must use words acquired within society while at the same time adopting a social scientific, outsider-like stance toward that society. Because words can be slippery, there is potential for confusion.

Jargon

Critics often ridicule sociologists for dressing their ideas up in unnecessarily complicated language—what has been called jargon or sociologese.[1] This critique suggests that sociologists' pretentious language is designed to conceal the fact that sociology is nothing more than common sense. Even sociologists criticize other camps within the discipline for using unnecessarily dense and arcane vocabulary.[2]

This critique can put sociologists on the defensive, and some will justify their prose by arguing that technical language is necessary to formulate ideas precisely. After all, chemists and other scientists use specialized vocabularies, surely sociologists have a right to select the words they use. But other sociologists are more likely to concede that jargon's critics have a point, and they call for clearer writing within the discipline.[3]

Sociologists' problems with language are not merely stylistic. There are real pitfalls in social scientific prose that can create logical problems for sociologists' reasoning. From its title, for instance, the book *Learn to Write Badly: How to Succeed in the Social Sciences* by social psychologist Michael Billig might seem to be just another complaint about jargon; however, he has a more important point: that the creation of neologisms encourages sociologists to equate these new words with actual explanations.[4] Typically this involves inventing nouns to describe social processes, such as *bureaucratization* or *modernization*. Watch how such a word can give the illusion of explanation. Suppose Ashley observes that societies change by adopting practices from other societies; since this typically involves becoming more like other societies we consider modern, she calls this process *modernization*. What is happening to Society X? It is modernizing. Why is it modernizing? Because it is becoming more like other modern societies.

Phrased this way, we can't help but recognize that this is a tautology—the fallacy of stating that A is true because we assume it to be true: Society X is modernizing because it is becoming more like other modern societies (which is the definition of modernization). But typically such usage is dressed up in more verbiage—for instance, declaring that Society X "is undergoing the process of modernization." This adds a passive verb—a grammatical device that often obscures just who is acting—and that totally useless "process of," redundant because modernization is itself by definition a process. What we end up with is the process of the process of becoming more like other modern societies—and it remains merely a description, not an explanation. Adding more words does not help Ashley actually explain anything.

Word Fads

Sociologists' vocabularies—like all language—have evolved over time. Words that were once popular have fallen out of favor, as new terms became fashionable. For instance, at the beginning of the twentieth century, *colored* was the polite, respectful term for people with dark skin whose ancestors came from Africa (thus the National Association for the Advancement of Colored People, or NAACP, founded in 1909). By midcentury, *colored* had fallen out of favor, and the term *Negro* was preferred (as in the National Negro College Fund, founded in 1944). By the late 1960s, *black* had supplanted *Negro* (the Congressional Black Caucus was founded in 1971). Later, *Afro-American* (briefly) and then *African American* gained traction.[5] At different times, people who were trying to be respectful applied these terms to the same group of people, and as each new term was adopted, its predecessors came to seem dated, discourteous, even disrespectful.

Consider a second example: in the late nineteenth century, the polite term used by professionals for those who were considered less intelligent was *feebleminded*. As psychologists began applying intelligence tests, they generated new terms, such as *moron* (defined as a person with a measured IQ between 51 and 70). By midcentury, *mentally retarded* replaced *moron* (as well as *imbecile* and *idiot*—also terms that denoted particular ranges of low IQ scores). The currently preferred term is *intellectually disabled*. All of these terms originally found favor among physicians, psychologists, and other experts; using them when they were shiny and new signaled an enlightened professionalism. But as they disseminated throughout the population, they took on derogatory connotations, and demand arose for a new, more dignified term. Using that new term marked you as someone who was respectful, just as continuing to use an older term suggested that you were out of touch, insensitive, even crass.

This pattern—something, for instance a new word, emerges and spreads, only to fade in popularity—is the hallmark of all fads.[6] Although we tend to associate fads with frivolity, even the most serious social worlds—including, yes, sociology—experience fads. Sociological vocabulary is very much a product of its time; new words are continually rising while old ones gradually vanish: *Oriental* becomes *Asian, gender* supplants *sex role,* and *language* turns into *discourse.* New concepts such as *compulsory heteronormativity* emerge. Some of these changes reflect shifts in the larger society's language, while others are restricted to the confines of sociology, even to particular sociological camps.

Notice that these word choices become status symbols. Sociologists—particularly those suffering from philosophy envy (see chapter 6)—who can toss around the current sophisticated lingo demonstrate to the world that they are up-to-date, on top of their discipline's most advanced thinking, while those who persist in using no-longer-fashionable terms reveal themselves to be behind the times, perhaps even implicated in the errors of the past. Authors—and editors—must make all sorts of decisions about the words they choose: What are you saying if you choose to write *black* as opposed to *Black*?[7] And if you choose *Black*, should you also write *White*? When you are talking about some general person, should you choose *he*, or *she*, or *he or she*, or *they*? Even such seemingly minor decisions can seem to reveal where you stand and affect how you and your ideas are judged by others.

Obviously, new terminology does not spread evenly everywhere or all at once. Rather, it travels along existing social networks. Within sociology, terms tend to emerge and initially spread within camps. Some never travel beyond the borders of a single camp, while others get adopted by other sociological camps, even by people outside sociology. The most successful terms make inroads with the media, government officials, and other visible figures who can serve as exemplars of correct usage. It is probably easier to change terms that designate smaller—as opposed to larger—categories of people, and more difficult to impose labels on others than for a group to demand a new label for itself. For example, as the term *African American* was displacing *black*, some suggested that whites should be relabeled *European Americans*, but that term never gained much traction. Similarly, the growing attention to transgender people has led those interested in gender issues to term people whose gender identities match their bodies' sexual organs as *cisgendered*. Whether that term—still relatively new when I wrote this—will be generally adopted remains to be seen, but since the word describes the vast majority of people, most of whom probably don't recognize a need for it, it seems unlikely that it will ever attain broad usage outside particular academic camps and social circles.

Words tend to be adopted because they prove useful. Most new words emerge as an effort to describe everyday life. I don't know who originated the term *helicopter parent*, but lots of folks adopted it. Other terms, such as *role model* or *significant other,* originated within sociology, only to spread into the general population, although most words that emerge within particular sociological camps do not—and should not be expected to—disseminate broadly, probably because they don't seem useful. As a consequence, the audience for sociological work is smaller than it might be if sociologists wrote in more accessible prose.

Definitions

Inventing concepts has an additional problem. Sociologists rarely define the terms they invent precisely enough that others can draw sharp boundaries around a concept's meaning, so as to say "*This* is an instance of this concept, but *that* is not."

Consider deviance, which sociologists began speaking of in the late 1940s. The interesting idea behind the concept was that there were similarities in the ways people thought about and treated crime, mental illness, suicide, and sexual relations outside of marriage. At first glance, these might seem to be different sorts of phenomena. For instance, people who committed crimes were considered responsible for their actions, while the mentally ill were not; as a result, criminals were punished, but the mentally ill were given treatment. In practice, however, there were similarities: the prisons that held convicted criminals and the mental hospitals that in those days held large numbers of mental patients—many of whom had been involuntarily committed—didn't seem all that different.[8]

And so sociologists began to explore what linked these phenomena, offering the concept of deviance. Initially they argued that deviance should be defined as the violation of a norm. This was pretty obvious in the case of criminals—a crime involved breaking a law. But what norms did the mentally ill violate? Is there really a *rule* that says we shouldn't be, say, severely depressed? Sociologists tried to get around this by explaining that mental illness involved breaking *residual rules* (which is to say, unwritten rules). But the various problems with the deviance-is-breaking-a-norm definition led to labeling theory, which defined deviance as whatever people considered "deviant." Of course, this was a term that people don't usually use in everyday life, so it was hard to know how to apply the concept. Sociologists have offered dozens if not hundreds of slightly different definitions of deviance since then, but at bottom most of those definitions agree that deviance involves breaking a norm and/or being labeled as deviant.

But the real problem is figuring out what the domain of deviance—however it may be defined—covers. Crime and mental illness—sure. Homosexuality? Once regarded as troubling (and routinely lumped into the category of deviance), not just homosexuality but all manner of sexual orientations are now regarded by most sociologists as outside the category of deviance. Similarly, early deviance textbooks contained chapters on other topics no longer covered in deviance courses, such as gambling, divorce, and premarital sex. Indeed, sociologists have identified all sorts of disparate phenomena as forms of deviance, including jazz musicians, redheads, the Holocaust, and disabilities. It is not clear what these have in common, which is to say, it is not clear how deviance has been defined. We can see similar confusion with other sociological concepts whose definitions lean heavily on arresting examples: "See," their authors seem to be saying, "this concept is illustrated by these examples."

Concept Creep

The problem with concepts built on vague definitions is that they can easily be applied to an ever larger array of subjects. This is often taken to be a sign of the concept's usefulness and its author's influence. Because an author who invents a term is supposed to be cited when some other careful researcher uses that term, such citations provide "evidence" that the author is an influential thinker, and that the concept is a useful one. All of this reinforces the tendency to adopt faddish words, which brings favorable attention to both their creators and the folks with-it enough to adopt them.

Such citations are easy when the concept itself has been vaguely defined. Take the example of deviance again. Everyone knows that righthanded people outnumber those who are lefthanded, and that lots of everyday objects such as wristwatches and scissors are designed in ways that make them easier for righthanded people to use. Why not argue that being lefthanded is a form of deviance? That links lefthandedness—a topic some (probably lefthanded) author might find interesting—with the larger body of sociological thought.

Notice that lefthandedness is rather different from crime and mental illness, the classic examples of deviance. Lefthanded people are not compelled to enter institutions that resemble prisons or mental hospitals. They simply suffer minor inconveniences in a world engineered for righthanded folks—it is harder for them to wind a watch or use scissors, and they might experience a bit of teasing. Now, it is possible to imagine a scale of social inconvenience ranging, say, from severe punishment to the mildest sort of disapproval, with career criminals placed at the imprisonment end and lefthanded people near the teasing end. Clearly, when sociologists began talking about deviance, they envisioned the concept as referring to people who were subject to severe sanctions such as imprisonment. But as time passed, and as other sociologists started including jazz musicians and redheads in the category of deviance, the concept's domain began to expand.

This is concept creep: over time what a concept is thought to encompass—begins to grow. There is no natural end to this process.[9] I have heard sociologists half-jokingly say, "Well, everyone is deviant." But if we take this remark seriously, it poses a problem. If everyone is deviant, then the meaning of deviance has morphed such that it is now synonymous merely with being human. The term has lost all value as a tool for thinking sociologically. Concept creep is the sociological equivalent of the economist's hyperinflation: a term can be used to refer to so many different things that it becomes nearly worthless.

Concept creep is encouraged by those fuzzy definitions we examined above. Sociologists tend to define their terms using examples, others are invited to add examples, and gradually, almost unnoticed, the new additions are less and less like the original examples that inspired the term in the first place.

Consider Erving Goffman's classic essay "On the Characteristics of Total Institutions." Goffman does not offer a precise definition, but notes that some institutions "are encompassing to a degree discontinuously greater than the ones next in line. Their encompassing or total character is symbolized by the barrier to social intercourse with the outside and to departure that is often built right into the physical plant, such as locked doors, high walls. . . . These establishments I am calling *total institutions*."[10] Goffman then goes on to list the sorts of places he means—prisons, mental hospitals, military bases, convents. The vague definition did Goffman's analysis no harm because his essay's examples were so compelling. As the concept of total institution grew increasingly influential, people began to apply the term to an ever broader array of settings, including high schools and colleges. We can see the attraction of doing so: calling a high school a total institution suggests that it is just like a prison, an entertaining notion that reminds us that at least some students feel imprisoned in school classrooms. And what about other settings where people may feel estranged or trapped? Places like shopping malls or theme parks? There is little to discourage an enthusiastic sociologist from including them within the domain of total institutions.

Imagine natural scientists adopting this approach. Suppose, for example, that chemists started saying that atoms with a couple more than eight protons could also be designated as oxygen. The idea is ridiculous. Rather, natural scientists police the boundaries of their concepts. When I was in elementary school, we learned that nine planets orbited the sun. In 2006, however, astronomers voted to reclassify Pluto as a dwarf planet, and today's schoolchildren learn that the solar system has eight planets. Pluto was demoted partly because it was unlike the remaining planets in its orbit and composition: whereas the inner four planets are basically rocks, and the outer four are giant balls of gas, Pluto is a small chunk of frozen matter. Astronomers were beginning to detect other smaller, even more distant icy lumps orbiting the sun. If Pluto was a planet, shouldn't these other objects also join the ranks of the planets? They decided to draw the line, to exclude Pluto from the list of planets rather than add lots of other small, uninteresting frozen chunks to that list.

Why do sociologists find it so difficult to control the edges of their concepts? It is not just that their definitions are unclear. There are advantages to piggybacking on a familiar, established concept. It allows the analyst to argue that whatever is being studying is like—similar to, essentially the same as, really no different from, the moral equivalent of—the established concept. It also lets the analyst take advantage of whatever prestige the existing concept has.

But there is a cost. If all arguments are intended to persuade, then they are a form of communication: the goal is to transfer ideas in one person's head to another person's brain. The words we choose make that easier or harder. Deciding to use obscure, arcane, unfamiliar sociologese may make the individual using such language feel smart or sophisticated, but it can discourage the intended audience from bothering to pay attention. And without clear definitions that constrict sociological concepts' domains, it is difficult for the discipline to make lasting progress.

Critical Thinking Takeaways

- Word choices can sometimes improve, sometimes distort, an argument's clarity.
- Words choices are subject to fads.
- Because sociological concepts are ill-defined, it is easy for their domains to expand.

9   *Questions and Measurements*

We may have all sorts of questions about the world: Does God exist? Why is the sky blue? What is fair? Can there be justice? and so on. It is important to recognize that sociology can help answer only some sorts of questions. Sociologists may have personal opinions about whether God exists, or remember enough of what they learned in basic science classes to explain why the sky is blue, but they are not drawing on their sociological expertise when they address those questions.

Sociological Questions

If the sociological perspective focuses on the effects people have on one another, then sociological *questions* address whether, why, or how such effects operate. In practice, therefore, while sociologists rarely pontificate about the existence of God or the blueness of the sky, they may well make declarations about what is fair or just. Some even declare that sociologists ought to dedicate themselves to fostering fairness or justice. However, their training in sociology does not qualify them to make authoritative judgments about what is fair or just.

Claims about fairness and justice are *value judgments*, dependent on personal values. Differences in these values often lead to debates about social policies. Consider those familiar hot-button issues that people endlessly argue about—guns, abortion, the death penalty, affirmative action, euthanasia, immigration, drugs. The participants in these debates tend to justify their positions in terms of values such as fairness, justice, morality, freedom, rights, and equality. (As explained in chapter 2, these are warrants in their arguments.) Often, people on opposing sides invoke the same values: both proponents and opponents of legal abortion, for example, justify their views using the language of rights (that is, a woman's right to choose vs. the fetus's right to life), just as debates over affirmative action turn to competing ideas of fairness. Values are abstractions, and people can invoke the same general value yet disagree about what that value means in practice.

Value judgments vary from time to time and place to place, and no one should be better aware of this than sociologists, who, after all, study cultural differences. Two centuries ago, there were Americans who insisted that slavery was fair, just, normal, and desirable, while at the same time there were other Americans who disputed all of those claims. What arguments people have used to support or oppose slavery at different points in time is the sort of thing that sociologists are interested in; it is very much their business to study how and why particular ideas about fairness or justice emerge, spread, or fade. In our era, the view that slavery is wrong is nearly universal. But declarations that slavery is bad, or claims that something is or is not fair or just, derive from an individual's personal values, not from sociology.

This fact can be obscured when people cite their credentials—as a professor of (some subject) at (some) university, say—when expressing their values or offering an opinion. Learning that a person of some standing holds some view may help persuade others toward that view. But we also need to consider the relevance of their credentials: physicians may be more qualified to speak to medical topics than laypersons, but their judgments will be most compelling when their professional specialty is relevant. Similarly, a sociology professor who signs a petition declaring a position on a nonsociological question should be understood to be speaking as a citizen, not as a sociologist.

Obviously, all sociologists—like all other people—have values. The idea of a perfectly value-free sociology is best understood as a goal, in that researchers should strive to honestly assess evidence, to not let their values distort what their research shows. In practice, however, values often shape what sociologists choose to study and even how they interpret their evidence.

Empirical Questions

Sociologists sometimes say, "That's an empirical question," meaning that it should be possible to answer by examining evidence from the real, empirical world. Let's take a simple example: imagine a college classroom filled with students. Adam wonders whether the class has more males than females. To find out, he might look in the classroom and simply count the numbers of males and females. The question of whether males outnumber females in the class is, then, an empirical one, and can be answered by examining evidence from observations.

Not all empirical questions are sociological, of course. It is presumably possible to test explanations for why the sky is blue, but sociological reasoning is not involved. Similarly, not all questions about sociological topics are necessarily empirical—or even socio-logical. Sociologists are quite interested in inequality but, as we have seen, people can frame questions about inequality—such as, "Is inequality fair?"—that lie outside sociology's domain. Sociologists can, however, collect evidence on the kinds, extent, and consequences of inequality, and we can ask empirical questions about those topics. Inequality can be studied sociologically, but sociology cannot determine whether inequality is right or wrong.

Measurement

Answering an empirical question requires that we devise some method for examining the evidence we collect, for measuring what we're trying to understand. Let's return to Adam's question. In this case, his method involved counting the students within two categories, male and female. Brenda, however, challenges this approach: What if some students were absent when he made his observations? Or perhaps some students' appearance is ambiguous, so that it is hard to confidently identify their sex? In other words, Adam's technique of looking at the classroom may not accurately measure the relative numbers of males and females. Chuck then suggests a different approach: just look at the class roster and tally up the male and female names. But, Debbie counters, Chuck's method is also problematic, because some first names, such as Adrian or Taylor, can be either male or female. If he could find a roster that gives each student's sex, that might work. Yet Ed objects that simply looking at the students or checking their names against a roster are both flawed because not everyone has a binary gender identity—some students may reject society's classifying them as either male or female.

And so on. The point is, every attempt to answer an empirical question requires some sort of procedure for collecting the necessary evidence and then for evaluating it. Anyone who has actually conducted a piece of research—even if it involved nothing more than counting the numbers of males and females in a classroom—has had to make choices, to decide what to examine and how to carry out that examination. And as the discussion among Adam and his pals reveals, it is always possible for people to second-guess those choices, to suggest reasons why a particular approach might not be the best way to gather evidence. Such debates revolve around two key issues: *validity*—will the proposed method actually measure what it is supposed to?— and *reliability*—can we count on the method to produce the same results each time we use it?

In Adam's case, labeling people as males or females is about as straightforward as measurement gets. In the vast majority of cases, the people being classified, the researcher, and the people who read the researcher's results are likely to view this male-female classification as relatively unproblematic. But things can get a lot trickier really fast.

Suppose Jones and Smith are opponents in an election, and you're a pollster who wants to see which candidate is ahead in order to project how the election is likely to turn out. Sounds simple, right? But there are all sorts of questions about the best way to measure public opinion about an election. Who should you survey? You could go to a shopping mall and ask the people you encounter there which candidate they prefer—but not everyone goes to that mall, and some people probably spend a lot more time there (and are therefore more likely to run into you) than others. To get more accurate results, you need some sort of *representative sample* of the population—in this case, of the people who live in the area where the election is being held. Getting such a sample is likely to be a lot more time-consuming and expensive than making a quick run to the mall, but assume you overcome those problems and come up with a reasonably representative sample of folks to interview. This is important because you want to be able to generalize—to argue that attitudes among the relatively few people you interview reflect the entire voting population.

Even with a representative sample, there will be measurement issues. You probably ought to ignore the responses of people in your sample who aren't eligible to vote, perhaps because they are underage or noncitizens. In addition, you probably should ignore respondents who, while they might be eligible, are not registered to vote. Serious pollsters go further: they try to determine who is *likely* to vote by asking respondents whether they plan to vote, whether they voted in the last election, and whether they know where their polling place is. Depending on which respondents you decide to include in reporting the survey results, the proportion favoring Jones and Smith might go up or down. Oh, and you'll need to decide what to do with the responses of people who say they haven't made up their minds or who refuse to respond because they figure their preference is none of your damn business.

All researchers confront such issues. Every measurement involves deciding both what it is that should be measured (the number of males and females in some class; levels of support for Jones vs. Smith) and how to go about that making that measurement (counting physical bodies or examining the class roster; choosing which respondents ought to be included in a survey). These choices can affect the research findings, which means detractors may question and criticize them. Inevitably, the method you choose may raise other questions, such as what to do if students are absent on the day you happen to make your observations, or how to weigh a respondent who hasn't voted in recent elections. That means more choices, and more possible criticism.

This is a good place to recall the basic principle of critical thinking: it is hardest to think critically about your own reasoning, your own choices. This is why sociology students are required to take courses in methodology, which discuss the advantages and disadvantages of different measurement techniques), and statistics, which focus on procedures for evaluating the measurements that are made. These courses basically offer guidance for making better measurement choices that should lead to more valid, reliable, and generalizable results. They emphasize the importance of understanding how one's choices can affect outcomes, and the need for both researchers and the people reading research reports to think critically about the measurements chosen.

Methods classes also teach that researchers have an obligation to describe those choices as part of their research reports, so that readers can assess whether the researcher has measured in ways that seem likely to have produced accurate results. Even news reports about polls, for example, are likely to give such basic information as the dates the poll was conducted, which respondents were included (registered voters? likely voters?), the number of respondents in the sample, and perhaps the wording of the questions asked. Such information can help readers judge how much confidence they should have in a poll's results.

What Is Being Measured?

All measurements involve compromise. Every research project costs time and money, which place practical constraints on a researcher's choices. But there are other sorts of compromises that bedevil researchers. Pick a topic that might be studied—say, crime. We're all used to hearing people talk about crime rates going up or down. But how do we measure crime? The answer might seem obvious: doesn't the FBI publish crime rate data in their Uniform Crime Reporting program? Still, such statistics are hardly perfect.[1] The FBI collects those data from local law enforcement agencies' reports of "crimes known to the police." In other words, if a crime occurs but no one reports it, meaning the local police never learn about it, then they can't report it to the FBI, which therefore can't include it in the crime rate. Many, many crimes thus go unrecorded. And there are lots of other problems, such as when a local police department fails to report some of the crimes that come to its attention. Why? Because underreporting gives the impression that the crime rate in their jurisdiction is lower than it actually is, which makes the department look better. Then too, not all jurisdictions submit reports to the FBI, nor does the crime rate include all crimes—and on and on. In other words, the crime rate as published by the FBI is a very imperfect measure.

These problems have led the federal government to try to measure crime a second way. The National Crime Victimization Survey (NCVS) is conducted by the Bureau of Justice Statistics. It asks a large sample of people whether they have recently been criminally victimized and whether they reported that crime to the police. About half the time, people who report having been victimized say they didn't report the crime, so NCVS victimization rates are higher than the FBI's crime rates.[2] But again, there are gaps in the information collected: the NCVS only asks about a few types of crime, respondents may simply refuse to acknowledge victimization, and of course the NCVS can't ask people whether they have been murdered.

Still, many researchers choose to use FBI or NCVS data. These data may be imperfect, but they are readily available and criminologists understand their limitations. Moreover, it is difficult to imagine how researchers could measure crime much more accurately. Compromise is inevitable: the available data may not be terrific, but they are the best we have.

This problem is very common. Often sociologists are interested in an abstraction such as crime, but there is no way to measure it directly. Consider, for example, research on fear of crime. Everyone has experienced fear at one time or another, and everyone has undoubtedly worried about crime. It is a short step to arguing that lots of people are quite concerned about crime, and to label this as "fear of crime."[3] But can we *measure* it? The solution offered by some criminologists is to conduct a survey. Many early studies were based on responses to the question "Is there any area right around here—that is within a mile—where you would be afraid to walk alone at night?" Notice that this question does not even include the word *crime;* the analysts simply assumed that a positive response to this question meant that respondents could be said to be experiencing fear of crime. How much confidence should we have in such an indirect measure?

Questioning Measurements

Precisely because, in the questions sociologists ask, measurements are imperfect, it is always possible for critics to question them.[4] Beyond simply noting flaws in the data, these critiques often argue that the researcher's measurement choices skew the findings in some way.

The national census offers a nice example. In theory, the census is supposed to count everyone, and the U.S. Census Bureau tries hard to produce a complete and accurate count. In practice, however, the census invariably fails to count some people, and the folks who don't get counted tend to be different from those who do. In particular, those who go uncounted tend to be poorer and members of ethnic minorities. Since census results are used to determine not just the number of seats each state has in the House of Representatives, but also the sums allocated to the states for various federal programs, undercounting has real consequences: states with lots of uncounted people stand to receive less power and money than they would if the census actually counted everyone. Complaints about the census are not simply that it falls short of the ideal of accurately counting every person, but that the undercounts advantage some while disadvantaging others.

Similar problems plague sociologists' measurement choices. This distortion need not be intentional; it may be unperceived or downplayed. Nor is there a simple way to resolve these problems. But a key to addressing the issue lies in critical thinking and transparency. Researchers must think carefully about the choices they make and the possible effects of those choices. They need to explain their decision-making process, including the rationales behind it. And they need to submit that information to others—peer reviewers and journal editors—who can evaluate the choices that were made.

And again, the social organization of sociology affects this process. Because sociological researchers tend to belong to particular camps, their research tends to appear in those camps' venues, which are overseen by editors and peer reviewers allied with those camps, which means that work is being judged by those sympathetic with the researcher's basic perspective. It is thus especially important that everyone involved in the process be willing to think critically about the research they are evaluating. These concerns continue as we move beyond measurement.

Critical Thinking Takeaways

- Sociologists' special qualifications are limited to sociological questions that address people's effects on one another.
- Empirical questions can be answered by collecting and evaluating evidence.
- All researchers make choices about the measurements they use when they gather evidence, and those choices may affect what they find.

10 *Variables and Comparison*

Because sociologists are insiders trying to analyze the society to which they belong, they must make an effort to distance themselves, to stand back from the culture and social structure they take for granted. Comparing aspects of social life becomes the key tool for achieving that distance, allowing them to discover and demonstrate what is happening. Comparison thus lies at the center of sociological reasoning.

Such comparisons can take various forms. Most basically, sociologists compare categories of people—males with females, the young with the old, rich with poor, or people of various ethnicities. They may also compare types of social arrangements, such as family structures, institutional organizations, or religions. Some focus on place, comparing social life in different neighborhoods, cities, or even nations, or on time, looking at everything from how people behave at different hours of the day to tracking social changes across centuries. Understanding the logic of such comparisons requires first considering the nature of variables.

Variables

A variable is anything that can have more than one value. Those values are chosen by the analyst: thus, the variable "height" might be split into two values—tall and short—or into many, by measuring height in inches or centimeters. Causal arguments involve at least two variables: the cause is called the *independent variable* because its value is independent of the effect's value. The independent variable is what changes to bring about an effect. That effect, in turn, is called the *dependent variable* because its value depends on the cause's value; the dependent variable is what is being measured. For instance, the position of a light switch up or down (the cause) is not affected by—is independent of—whether the light bulb is glowing (the effect). However, whether the light bulb glows does depend on the switch being flipped.

Take a simple argument: the more students study, the higher the grades they receive; here, how much students study is the independent variable, and the grades they receive is the dependent variable. Suppose we decide to test this by comparing the grades on a twenty-point spelling test of (a) those students who studied more than one hour and (b) those who studied less than one hour. Table 1 shows what we might find. Right away we can see how different values of the independent variable—in this case, more and less study time—lead to different effects.

TABLE 1 Average of Students' Scores on Spelling Test by Amount of Time Spent Studying

Studied more than one hour	Studied less than one hour
17.9	14.4

If we are trying to understand what causes some dependent variable—say, crime—we could compare all sorts of independent variables; for example: Do males commit more crimes than females? Do those who attend religious services regularly commit fewer crimes than nonattenders? Are residents of cities more likely to commit crimes than people living in suburbs? Are more crimes committed in daytime or at night? In each case, the comparison is between different values of the independent variable—sex, religious attendance, type of neighborhood, time of day.

TABLE 2 Average of Students' Scores on Spelling Test by Amount of Time Spent Studying and Whether They Listened to Music while Studying

Listened to Music	Amount studied	
	More than one hour	Less than one hour
No	18.3	15.6
Yes	16.2	12.8

However, there is a third kind of variable: an *intervening variable*. Intervening variables alter the cause's impact on the effect. Suppose someone takes the results of our research on test scores and decides to examine how listening to music while studying affects the relationship between independent (amount of time spent studying) and dependent (test scores) variables. Table 2 shows what we find. This new study controls for listening to music—the intervening variable—by comparing four groups of students: (1) those who studied more than one hour without listening to music; (2) those who studied more than one hour while listening to music; (3) those who studied less than one hour without listening to music; and (4) those who studied less than one hour while listening to music. In this case, both the independent and intervening variables are subject to comparison. Here we find that more time spent studying improved the students' spelling test scores, but that no matter how much time is spent studying, listening to music while doing so leads to somewhat lower scores.

Issues with Comparison

In short, sociologists compare. Many of their comparisons explore differences in the lives of familiar categories of people. This makes it is easy to gloss over the complexities involved in making useful comparisons. Let's look at two fundamental issues.

The first set of issues are methodological. Recall chapter 8's discussion of measurement. In order to compare categories of people, we need to be able to define the criteria we will use to place people in one category or another. This turns out to be trickier than it might seem. For instance, while researchers have long assumed that it is possible to ask folks to classify themselves as either male or female—categories that continue to fit how the vast majority of people think of themselves—we increasingly find questionnaires that invite people to choose their gender from among a larger array of options. And of course, most of the variables sociologists employ involve far less clear-cut measurements than gender. Take social class. Does it refer to income (the amount of money people make)? Or it is really about wealth (the value of what people own)? Or is it about occupation (remembering that some farmers and some lawyers make lots of money, even as other farmers and lawyers earn relatively little)? Or is it about how much education one has? The answer to each of these questions—unsatisfying as this might be—is "Well, yeah, sort of . . . " Most sociologists acknowledge that class is multifaceted, that lots of people seem to straddle social class boundaries, by, for example, being highly educated yet having a relatively low income. However interesting such anomalous cases might be, when sociologists are trying to do actual research, they usually don't have the time to painstakingly parse the class of each person in the study. Instead, they tend to use some simple, quick-and-dirty measure—such as household income, or parents' educational attainment—to categorize people by class.

In other words, categorizing people is inevitably imperfect and subject to question. This leads to a second set of issues, and these are related to theory—the reasoning underlying the methodology. Typically, the opening paragraphs in a sociological research report justify a particular comparison by arguing that it answers—or at least contributes to answering—some question raised by sociological theory. In effect, the author maintains that the project is worthy of the reader's attention because the comparison can help us learn something we might want to know. A reader always has the right to ask an author, "So what?" The explanation that this research poses a theoretically interesting question is a way of addressing that challenge.

Varieties of Comparative Findings

Imagine a four-cell table that classifies researcher's expectations into two groups—a prediction that the comparison will reveal a difference and a prediction that it will show no difference—and divides each of those according to the research findings—those that show a difference and those that do not. (See table 3.) The four cells in this table represent research outcomes. In the cell labeled A, the researcher predicted that some comparison would reveal a differ-

TABLE 3 Researchers' Expectations and Possible Outcomes

	Researcher's hypothesis	
Actual findings	Difference expected	No difference expected
Difference found	A	D
No difference found	B	C

ence, and that difference was found. For the researcher, this is the ideal situation; sociology journals are filled with articles in which authors develop theories, derive hypotheses that can be tested through some sort of comparison, and then report results demonstrating that the results were as hypothesized. This result seems encouraging because it suggests that the authors' theory may be correct, and that it would be worthwhile to explore that theory further.

The B cell ought to be important. These are cases where the sociologist predicts that there will be a difference, yet the results fail to demonstrate one. This suggests that the sociologist's reasoning may be incorrect, that the world does not work the way the researcher thought it did, or possibly that the theory behind the hypothesis is mistaken. In principle, negative results such as this are important because they reveal a theory's failure to predict correctly. However, analysts usually have a stake in believing their reasoning to be sound, and they may be reluctant to junk their theory simply because this study failed to support its predictions. Instead, they may favor other possible interpretations. Perhaps the sociologist did not design the research well, making it unable to properly test the theory's predictions. Perhaps a better analytic technique, such as a more sophisticated statistical test, would have led to results more consistent with the theory's predictions. Perhaps the theory is generally correct but needs to be amended to cover the study's results. In other words, there is a tendency to give the theory the benefit of the doubt in the face of one unconfirmed prediction.

In practice, type-B negative results are difficult to publish. While a journal editor will gladly accept type-A research that confirms theoretical hypotheses, negative results tend to be blamed not on the theory but on the researcher, who, critics suspect, most likely did something wrong. Of course, if several researchers get negative results, support may grow for the idea that the theory is somehow flawed. But in the short run, there is inertia in favor of considering theories viable until substantial evidence suggests otherwise.

Journal editors' reluctance to publish negative results has real consequences. Suppose ten different studies have been launched to determine whether a new pharmaceutical drug is more effective than the existing treatment, and in nine of the ten studies the new drug fails to outperform. Those type-B studies will probably not be published (particularly if the research was funded by the pharmaceutical company that developed the drug, which will have little interest in reporting disappointing findings).[1] Meanwhile, the single type-A study that suggests the new drug is effective finds its way into print, thereby becoming the only public word on the matter. That, then, will be all that anyone searching the scientific literature on the subject will find: support for the new drug's superiority.

The cells on the right side of the table pose somewhat different issues. For one thing, it is relatively uncommon (and not very interesting) to predict that no difference will be revealed in a comparison. The C cell pattern is less common, because it is usually harder to argue that predicting that a comparison will show no difference is interesting. However, sociologists sometimes use such an argument to challenge commonly held but potentially erroneous perceptions. For instance, imagine a widespread stereotype that one ethnic group is more prone to delinquency than another. A sociologist might argue that the apparent relationship between ethnicity and delinquency may be spurious, that in fact it is differences in social class that affect likelihood of becoming delinquent, and then go on to predict that apparent correlations between delinquency and ethnicity will disappear if we control for social class. The sociologist, then, might predict that there will be no differences—that the better-off members of both ethnic groups have equally low delinquency rates, just as less well-off members have equally high rates of delinquency. In such cases, finding no differences across ethnicity, but only between social classes, may be of interest—and in line with sociologists' predictions, such that editors prove receptive to publishing.

The fourth D cell is a little more complicated. These are cases where no difference is expected, and yet a difference is found. Above I suggested that no-difference predictions are often used to challenge conventional thinking. Yet type-D results that contradict researchers' no-difference predictions draw responses that resemble the responses to type-B results: they may be considered flawed and inconclusive.

There is, as I observed above, a tendency for researchers—and for the people who review their work—to be more invested in the theoretical reasoning than in the actual results of their research. A theory offers a framework, a tool for making sense of a multitude of observations. There is a natural reluctance to toss a valued theory out with the bathwater of disappointing research results. Not only that, but theoretical perspectives form the basis for important intellectual camps within sociology. In the face of research results that fail to confirm a theory's predictions, many of a camp's members are likely to explain away the troubling findings in order to keep the theory afloat.

Replication

We tend to think of research in terms of single, decisive studies: someone designs a key experiment that produces a dramatic finding. Media reports about scientific breakthroughs foster this impression.

In practice, science moves more slowly than this. Skeptics may challenge a finding and insist on replicating the study. The basic idea of replication is that repeating the same steps should produce the same results—for instance, every time we mix equal amounts of two clear liquid chemicals, the combination turns blue. If the result is different we know that something else must be going on, and we'd have to figure out what that might be. It can take time to conduct thorough research, which is why we should be skeptical when the news media announce a dramatic scientific breakthrough. Until a result has been convincingly replicated, any single finding should be considered tentative. Research reports need to be checked, evaluated, and ideally replicated.

In practice, it is difficult to replicate social scientific research. To take a familiar example, it is not uncommon for commentators to express frustration when election polls produce different results. How, they ask, can one poll have Candidate Jones ahead, while a second poll shows Candidate Smith in the lead? We already know from chapter 8's discussion of measurement that there are lots of reasons why this might happen. For instance, different polls may question different sorts of people: one poll may include the responses of all adults, including those not registered to vote; a second may only count the responses of registered voters; a third may include only those the pollsters define as likely voters (i.e., people who say they are likely to vote or who usually vote in elections). Or pollsters may word their questions in different ways, or they may have conducted their polls on different days. And, of course, all polls are samples; although they are designed to accurately represent the larger electorate, statistical theory tells us we must expect some variation in results among samples. All this means that the results of replication in social science are going to be less clear-cut than some combination of chemicals turning blue every time.

Moreover, sociological research rarely asks questions as straightforward as which candidate is in the lead for the upcoming election. It is usually possible to imagine all sorts of intervening variables that might affect the comparison a sociologist is making, and critics are likely to suggest that key intervening variables— ones that might dramatically affect the results—have been ignored.

Comparison in Qualitative Research

Thus far we have been considering fairly traditional sorts of social scientific reasoning, usually associated with quantitative analysis (hypotheses, independent and intervening variables, etc.) But what about qualitative research?

Suppose Austin spends two years observing how hospital emergency room staff deal with people who have been in automobile accidents. Why do this? Perhaps he is interested in comparing ER work, where urgent, high-pressure, high-stakes decisions are the norm, with more routine jobs. Or perhaps his focus is on how the work changes from weekday daytime shifts, when lots of other medical offices are open, to weekend nights, when more people with medical problems show up in the ER—that is, he's comparing differences in the ER workers' shifts. Or maybe he is interested in the differences between a big-city ER and one in a rural community.

There are many other possibilities, but whichever Austin chooses, he will likely be making explicit or implicit comparisons. Anyone who considers reading Austin's work can certainly ask, "Why should I spend a chunk of my life reading about people working in an ER?" After all there are countless settings that Austin could decide to observe, so why choose this one? Although it may not seem obvious at first, the answer to those questions always involves comparative thinking. Qualitative researchers often begin their research with a less clear-cut sense of what they are up to than sociologists who do quantitative research. After all, the first step in a quantitative study is to define the relationships the investigator intends to reveal. In contrast, qualitative research can involve exploration and discovery; qualitative researchers' descriptions of their methodology often acknowledge that they initially weren't quite sure what their focus would be, but once they began observing, they found themselves thinking that some aspect of the setting was interesting. That's the key step: recognizing that something seems interesting to you, and then figuring out why it should interest other people.

For qualitative researchers, comparisons are most powerful when there are a lot of examples. Much qualitative research involves a lone researcher observing some scene or interviewing people. An obvious criticism for such work is that that scene or those people may not be typical. A way to counter this is to demonstrate repeated occurrences of a particular behavior or set of circumstances: "I witnessed people doing Y on numerous occasions" or "Several of the people I spoke to said Z."

It also helps to find patterns among apparently similar observations or interviews. For instance, imagine that whenever a researcher saw a particular kind of person (call this Type X) in a certain situation, the subjects behaved in a similar way, whereas other kinds of people seen in that situation behaved differently. The researcher might suspect the behavior is related to Type X people.

Alternatively, our researcher might look for similarities among a range of apparently different observations or interviews. If Type X people were seen behaving in a distinctive manner in all sorts of very different situations, this, too, would suggest that those behaviors are characteristic of Type X. And so on. Ultimately, qualitative research depends on assembling a large set of comparisons, sufficient to demonstrate that some sort of pattern exists.[2]

Questioning Comparisons

In chapter 8 we noted that all researchers make choices regarding what they measure and how they go about making those measurements. Similarly, all researchers choose the comparisons they will make and, like measurements, those comparisons are subject to criticism.

Ideally, comparisons should be revealing: they should help us identify and understand patterns in the world—students who study more get better grades, Candidate Smith's support is concentrated among this group of voters; ER workers deal with the stress of their jobs in these ways. Effective comparisons convince readers that the sociologist's interpretations have weight.

When comparisons are critiqued, the charge often is that the researcher's choices were misguided. Critics of quantitative analyses, for example, may argue that the researcher failed to take an additional, and critical, intervening variable into account. Thus, the tobacco industry long argued that although there might *seem* to be a relationship between smoking and, say, cancer, the real culprit might in fact be alcohol or coffee or . . . you name it. Or in contemporary sociology, critics sometimes argue that analysts have failed to consider how race or gender might affect the apparent findings. A second, more technical sort of critique of quantitative comparisons is that the analyst should have chosen a different methodological design or a more sophisticated statistical test.

Critics of qualitative research also argue that appropriate comparisons have been overlooked. They may also argue that the setting chosen for observation or the people selected to be interviewed were somehow atypical, or that the researcher misinterpreted what was seen or said. Qualitative research is particularly vulnerable to critiques of evidence, because it is usually impossible to replicate such studies; any replication will inevitably deal with different research subjects at different times. Even if it is possible to approach the same subjects, those people are themselves presumably different, if only because they have already had the experience of being studied.

All research is rooted in the idea of comparison, and all comparisons reflect choices, which means that all comparisons can be criticized. There is no way to avoid this; researchers can only explain their choices and point to their evidence,

Critical Thinking Takeaways

- Causal arguments involve comparing values of independent and intervening variables.
- Whether research findings match researchers' expectations affects the response to those findings.
- Replication is difficult in the social sciences.
- All comparisons reflect choices that can be questioned.

11   *Tendencies*

The previous chapter began with the observation that sociologists compare categories of people, then went on to examine the logic of comparison. This chapter will consider what it means to understand the patterns that emerge within and between categories of people. Sociological thinking compares people belonging to all sorts of categories: males with females, whites with blacks, young with old, Californians with Texans, people who lived in the nineteenth century with those alive in the twenty-first century—the possibilities are endless.

Patterned Tendencies

When sociologists report the findings of their comparisons, they almost invariably describe them in terms of tendencies: people in Group A tend to be more (or less) likely to behave or think in some way than people in Group B.

It is important to appreciate what this means. Physical scientists sometimes are able to describe things that are always true: oxygen atoms have eight protons; or whenever we mix these two clear liquids, the result will be blue. But even they often find themselves talking about tendencies. Thus, we all know there is a vast amount of evidence that smoking causes lung cancer. But this is still a tendency: it does not mean that every single smoker will get the disease; in fact, only a small minority of smokers develop lung cancer. Nonetheless, smokers are much more likely than nonsmokers to develop lung cancer, and the vast majority of people who do succumb to it are current or former smokers. This is why, if we learn that Lucy has lung cancer, our first question is often, "Did she smoke?" But of course, sometimes the answer is no, she didn't; after all, some nonsmokers come down with the disease as well. Identifying the tendency for smokers to develop lung cancer means neither that all smokers will contract the disease, nor that everyone with the disease has smoked.

Understanding tendencies requires that we think probabilistically. Here, the classic examples come from games of chance involving flipping coins, rolling dice, or dealing cards. These are easily understood: if you flip a fairly balanced coin, there is a 50 percent chance it will come up heads; flip two coins, and there is a 25 percent chance both will be heads. This is because there is a 50 percent chance that the first coin will land heads, and on 50 percent of those occasions, the second coin will also show heads (.5 × .5 = .25). It is nearly as simple to determine that rolling one fairly balanced, six-sided die will show one dot one-sixth (16.67 percent) of the time; if you roll two dice, the chance that both will come up ones is 2.78 percent (.1667 × .1667 = .0278), or once every thirty-six rolls. These are neatly bounded examples; the whole point of dice is to produce a random outcome on each roll, yet we know that this will produce clear patterns if we roll them enough times. Thus, on average, for every thirty-six rolls of two dice, we should get a total of two once, while we can expect to get some combination of seven (1 + 6, 2 + 5, 3 + 4) six times in all.

While it is possible to apply probabilistic thinking to the patterns in people's lives, we know that social life is not neatly bounded. Insurance provides a relatively clear example. Insurance companies employ actuaries, people who calculate the odds of bad things happening—such as auto accidents, fires, or deaths—and then set rates based on those odds. Most drivers won't have a costly accident in the coming year, but some will, and the insurance company is willing to take your bet: you pay a premium and they promise to pay off if you have a costly accident. Actuaries know that some drivers, such as experienced drivers who aren't too old, or people who haven't received a lot of tickets, are less likely to get in accidents, and so the insurance company can charge those low-risk drivers lower premiums. There are a couple hundred million drivers in the United States, so actuaries have plenty of data with which to work. They can't know precisely *which* drivers will have an accident this year, but they wouldn't be surprised to learn that Xavier was not involved in an accident this year, or that Wanda was. The point is, they have a pretty good idea about the general pattern— what the total number of accidents will be—and that allows them to calculate appropriate premiums. This is little different than a casino knowing the odds of different outcomes in dice games and setting a payoff structure that insures that in the long run it will make a profit—except that the odds calculated by actuaries are not as precise as those for games of chance.

In effect, when sociologists conduct research and identify patterns (for instance, that this category of people is more likely to do X than some other category of people), they are producing very crude data of the sort that provides the basis for casinos' and actuaries' calculations. Notice that actuaries can draw upon various sources for their data—such as police reports of traffic accidents and insurance claim records from previous years—to predict how many accidents will occur in the coming year. Sociologists usually work with much less data—often just what they have themselves collected—so any estimates they make are likely to be much rougher than the actuaries' forecasts.

But just as actuaries use their data to predict the number of traffic accidents, which then serves as a basis for calculating reasonable premiums, sociologists use their findings to make generalizations about patterns in social life. To be sure, they cannot confidently predict precisely how Sarah will act, but they can describe a pattern based on the behavior of people in the category that Sarah belongs to.

This is why sociologists become impatient with people who use anecdotes to discount their findings. Imagine a sociologist whose research shows that older people tend to have conservative political beliefs. In response, Paul says, "That's not true—my grandma and grandpa are very liberal." This might be a telling critique if our sociologist had said that *all* older people are conservative. In that case, finding even one contradictory example would be enough to challenge the claim. But in identifying a *tendency* for older people to be conservative, the sociologist acknowledges that there will be some liberals among older people as well. Discovering that this particular older person is liberal does not destroy the sociologist's argument, any more than Xavier's not having a traffic accident discredits the actuaries' predictions for total number of collisions.

When sociologists attempt to strengthen their findings, they often—as discussed in the previous chapter—search for the effects of intervening variables. Our sociologist might check to see whether social class makes a difference in older people's political beliefs—and find that, indeed, older people of higher social class are more likely to be conservative than those of lower social class.

And so on. That is, it may be possible to be more specific about the patterns being determined, but still these findings will be expressed in terms of tendencies.

The Ecological Fallacy

Confusion about categories and tendencies takes a more complicated form in what sociologists call the *ecological fallacy*.[1] The basic idea here is that the categories sociologists compare are composed of individuals who behave in various ways. When sociologists report a measurement for a category, these measurements describe tendencies that will not fit all of its individuals. It is an error to assume that the tendency for some category describes individuals within that category. For instance, you can go online and find states ranked according to the percentage of college graduates in their populations.[2] These data come from the American Community Survey (a very large survey conducted by the U.S. Census Bureau), which asks individuals about their educational attainment. In 2017, Massachusetts had the highest percentage of adults who had completed at least a four-year college degree (43.4 percent), while West Virginia had the lowest (20.2 percent). In this example, the comparison is between percentages (college graduates) in two categories (states).

The ecological fallacy involves the following sort of reasoning:

Relatively few people in West Virginia hold college degrees.
Jack lives in West Virginia.
Therefore, Jack has not completed college.

The problem is that this assumes that a measurement for a category can be used to determine some characteristic of an individual member of that category. Phrased in this way, the problem is apparent: Jack might or might not have completed college; just because he lives in a state with relatively fewer college graduates does not allow us to conclude that he did not complete college.

Notice that this is different from saying:

Every member of the sociology faculty at West Virginia University (WVU) holds a college degree.
Jill is a member of the WVU sociology faculty.
Therefore, Jill has completed college.

In cases where all members of a category share some characteristic, we can safely conclude that an individual member in that category has that characteristic. However, sociologists rarely deal with such absolutes—with cases where everyone (or no one) in a category has some characteristic. In practice, sociologists deal in tendencies.

A version of the ecological fallacy also occurs when sociologists report a category's tendency in terms of an average. Let's say that (1) the average household income in some neighborhood is $60,000, and (2) Tim lives in that neighborhood. Knowing these two facts cannot allow us to conclude anything about the income of Tim's household—it might be higher, lower, or exactly the same as the average.

While these examples may seem obvious, it is easier to fall into the ecological fallacy when they examine patterns in two tendencies within categories. Recall that, in 2017, Massachusetts had the highest percentage of college graduates, while West Virginia had the lowest. Now suppose we look at another variable—say, reports of hate crimes. In 2017, Massachusetts reported 427 hate crimes, while West Virginia had only 31 such reports.[3] Because hate-crime statistics are notoriously inaccurate, the FBI does not calculate crime rates based on these reports—but if they had, it would work out to 6.4 reports per 100,000 people for Massachusetts, compared to only 1.9 for West Virginia. So we can see that Massachusetts has both more college graduates and more reported hate crimes, while West Virginia has fewer of both.

Where does the ecological fallacy come in? Imagine someone looks at our data and says, "Wow—the more college graduates, the more hate crimes. College graduates must be the ones committing hate crimes." In other words, we once again are using data about categories (percentage of college graduates, number of reported hate crimes) to draw conclusions about individuals in those categories (hate crimes must be committed by college graduates).

It is easy to see why this is an erroneous conclusion. Enforcement of hate crime laws varies wildly from state to state and jurisdiction to jurisdiction. States define hate crimes differently, and law enforcement agencies vary in how aggressively they enforce these statutes. In 2017, for example, seven states—Alabama, Alaska, Arkansas, Mississippi, Nevada, New Mexico, and Wyoming—each reported fewer than ten hate crimes. Generally speaking, more liberal states tend to have more expansive hate-crime laws, and prosecutors in more liberal jurisdictions tend to be more willing to charge individuals with hate crimes. Massachusetts has both a highly educated population and a liberal government; the state's high rate of reported hate crimes probably says more about the political environment within which its hate-crime laws are enforced than it does about the actual rate of hate crimes in the state.

The ecological fallacy can be seductive, particularly when its reasoning seems to support some conclusion that the analyst is predisposed to believe. At first glance, the logic may seem reasonable, and a number of prominent early (that is, pre–World War II) sociologists fell into this error before the problem was well understood. It remains something to watch for whenever we try to use data about categories to explain individuals' behavior.

The Modesty of Sociological Explanations

Typically, the tendencies that sociologists identify are not particularly powerful—the variables they study can rarely be treated as *the* cause of some effect. Knowing, say, that individuals who spent their childhood and adolescence living in households with their married parents may be more likely to complete college than those raised in other sorts of households is a tendency. But there will be lots of exceptions: people raised in two-parent households who drop out of school; people raised in single-parent households who excel in school; and so on.

Often sociologists use statistics to show the strength of the tendencies they identify. They may, for example, offer measures of the explained variation—basically, the proportion of the difference in outcomes that can be explained knowing just the tendency that research has identified. For example, what percentage of individuals' chances of completing college can be explained by knowing only that type of family household tends to affect educational attainment? Once again, having results that can be reported as statistically significant does not necessarily mean that the tendencies reported are especially visible to people living their lives. It is not uncommon for sociologists' results to explain only about 10 percent of the variation.

The danger here is that researchers may exaggerate the importance of their findings—in this case, to casually announce that they have established that family household is a cause of educational success. Such bold language blurs the fact that sociologists are, again, describing tendencies.

Thinking about Tendencies

Thinking in terms of tendencies or probabilities is both a powerful and a frustrating way of reasoning. Its power comes from the ability to discern and describe processes that may not be obvious at first glance—such as the realization that smoking substantially increases health risks, even if some smokers do not become ill. But the frustration follows from the realization that sociologists can rarely say that something is *the* cause of some effect. This is why exploring the effects of intervening variables is so central to sociological reasoning.

Critical Thinking Takeaways

- Sociologists identify tendencies when they compare categories of people.
- Knowing a tendency within a category is not enough to draw conclusions about individual members of that category.

12 *Evidence*

Researchers' choices extend far beyond measurement and comparison. Once the researcher has gathered and analyzed the evidence—which can range anywhere from quickly tallying the numbers of male and female students in a class to assessing field notes from years of observations in an emergency room—it is necessary to present the results. This can be a simple, straightforward matter, something along the lines of "While looking into the classroom, I counted X male and Y female students." However, most research is far more complex. For starters, research often involves collecting more data than will be reported. Pollsters know that most of the costs of conducting a survey lie in locating and contacting the respondents. As a result, it is expensive to ask just one question of a sample of people; but it adds very little to the cost to ask another question, or even several more (right up until too many questions become annoying and respondents start cutting short the interviews). Most pollsters, for instance, probably start with background characteristics such as the respondent's sex, age, and race, and they may then ask other substantive questions, such as whether they voted in the last election and whether they intend to vote in the next one. It is important to collect any data you think might be useful; if you later think of a question you wish you'd asked, it will be too late.

Once you've collected all these results, you'll have to decide what to report. If the poll's purpose was to determine whether likely voters favored candidate Jones or Smith in the coming election, you could of course report only that information. But as long as more information is available, you might decide to make use of it. Suppose after examining the results you realize that female voters and younger voters are much more likely to favor Jones, while Smith has greater support among older males. That might strike you as worth reporting.

The need for such choices becomes much more apparent when the research data take the form of extensive field notes or transcripts of interviews that may total many hundreds of pages. Many qualitative researchers use special software to comb through their data and help them identify themes and patterns. But at some point the researcher will be forced to decide which evidence seems relevant and worth writing up, based on a specific argument the researcher hopes to make.

Effective Evidence

Effective evidence supports the researcher's argument in a way others find convincing. In sociology, such arguments usually identify some pattern in how people affect one another, and they may focus on particular issues, such as which people are involved or how those effects occur. The role of evidence is to convince readers that the researcher's argument is correct. Several qualities make evidence effective.

On Point

At its best, evidence speaks directly to the researcher's claim: "I know—because I counted—the numbers of males and females in that class, and here are the data." This is a direct answer to the question the researcher sought to answer.

Unfortunately, most research addresses more complicated topics. A researcher's question may be somewhat abstract, such as whether a specific practice—police arrest procedures, standardized testing, etc.—is discriminatory. This is less straightforward than it might seem. To determine whether some practice is discriminatory, it will be necessary to define discrimination and describe how it will be measured. Recall our discussion of measurement in chapter 9. Effective evidence should speak directly to the issue being studied, and the measurements used must be clear and to the point.

Multiple Measures

In general, more evidence is better than less. Because measurement choices can always be questioned, evidence will be more convincing if it includes alternative measures that show consistent results. Survey researchers often ask multiple, slightly different questions on related topics. If the answers to these questions reveal a similar pattern, the evidence gains weight. For instance, consider a survey that asks about various environmental issues; if the younger respondents' answers to different questions consistently display higher levels of concern than the responses of older people, it would not be unreasonable to conclude that environmental concern is related to age.

Multiple Cases

Another way to produce more evidence is to study multiple cases. This is the basic idea behind replication: we found something interesting when we did the study, and we repeated the study to make sure that we got the same result.

In sociological research, multiple cases are often built into a study as a means of comparison. That is, the researcher compares the results from two or more schools, cities, time periods, or groups. When these comparisons produce similar results across the categories being compared, this strengthens the findings, and when the results show differences, explaining these may clarify the processes that are at work.

Consistent with Theory or Other Findings

Evidence is considered stronger if it appears to support widely accepted theories or previous research findings. That said, the history of science features a variety of ideas that encountered resistance at first, primarily because they contradicted familiar, widely accepted theories; two relatively recent examples are the idea that the earth's continents once belonged to a single land mass and gradually separated, and that the extinction of the dinosaurs was caused by an asteroid striking earth. Both proposals originally struck many scientists as outlandish, but over time, as findings from various studies proved consistent with the new theories, they achieved scientific respectability. In other words, although evidence that is consistent with existing theory tends to be readily accepted, in cases where evidence seems to point to an unexpected conclusion, support for the new idea may emerge over time as other studies corroborate the notion.

Compelling

Effective evidence makes a strong, convincing impression. Perhaps the study seems designed to have anticipated all obvious criticisms, thus circumventing familiar pitfalls; perhaps the research topic is especially interesting, raising a question people may not have thought about, or the way the topic is being studied seems especially clever; or perhaps the evidence being presented is so thorough that there seems no point in questioning it. For reasons such as these, some research has a disproportionate impact.

Not-So-Effective Evidence

Evidence can, however, be less effective, in ways that mirror each of the standards mentioned above.

Indirect

Whereas effective evidence is on point, in that it directly and thoroughly addresses the research question, ineffective evidence provides only imperfect support. Sometimes the only evidence available is indirect. For instance, social historians seeking to study how crime rates have changed over the centuries must confront the problem that modern police forces only arose in the nineteenth century, and modern crime rates—like those presented in the FBI's Uniform Crime Reports—only began being calculated in the twentieth. Therefore, there are no earlier crime records equivalent to those we now use to calculate crime rates. While it is possible to locate some court records that go back to the thirteenth century, these raise all sorts of other problems; many records have not survived, for starters, but the big problem is that most crimes never led to trials for which records were kept. A solution is to focus on homicides—which often did lead to trials, and to records being kept.[1] As a result, historians of crime wind up (of necessity) assuming that fluctuations in homicide rates—calculated from imperfect records—parallel change in general crime rates.

Such compromises are often unavoidable. It may not be possible to directly address the question that interests us with the evidence that is available. This is almost always true when we are trying to make comparisons with the past, when the data we might wish we had are simply not available. But it is also the case whenever data are hard to come by, as when the people being studied are reluctant to reveal what we'd really like to know.

Single Measures

Having multiple measures can make a researcher's case more persuasive, but again, these are not always available. Perhaps the responses to a single survey question on a topic show an unexpected, interesting result. In retrospect, the researcher might wish that additional questions on the topic had been asked, but of course it is now too late. Single measures may be suggestive, but until further research supports a finding, people may be reluctant to accept it.

Single Cases

Evidence from single cases tends to be viewed as less strong. A study based on observations in one neighborhood, for example, will inevitably raise questions: perhaps the findings only apply to that neighborhood and cannot be generalized. The researcher may strengthen the argument by documenting multiple cases within the neighborhood, but stronger support will depend on other researchers eventually reporting similar findings in other places. More evidence is always better than less evidence.

Inconsistent with Theory or Methods

As noted above, findings that seem to stand alone, that lack support from theory or other studies, tend to face suspicion. Ultimately, they may be proven correct, but only after considerably more support emerges. Moreover, the contemporary research literature is vast, with many new reports appearing every week. No one can hope to keep up with all of it. Most people therefore settle for trying to be more or less aware of what's happening in their own camps, but this means they are often oblivious to what is going on in other camps. Research that might be relevant to them, but that appears in a different camp's journal, may not have the impact it deserves. On a related note, because citations are a way of signaling to prospective readers that a paper is relevant to their concerns, research reports that fail to cite works by another camp's members may never gain attention in that camp.

Unimpressive

In a world where vast amounts of new research are continually appearing, most studies attract little attention. No sociologist can hope to keep track of every new book, let alone every article published in every journal. As a result, much gets lost along the way. People may ignore research that seems predictable, uninteresting, or irrelevant to their interests. At most, a sociologist can try to keep track of only a handful of journals, and then only by glancing at the table of contents. A given article can be easily overlooked, so even research that is well done winds up making little impression.

Questioning Evidence Choices

Like their measurement and comparison choices, researchers' choices about handling evidence can become targets for criticism. In most cases, it is assumed that researchers have honestly reported what they've found. Occasionally, however, scandals emerge when people call evidence into question, perhaps accusing someone of citing a nonexistent source or misrepresenting what a source says, of miscalculating a statistic, or of plagiarizing someone else's work. Such challenges tend to be worded carefully, and the author of the work is given an opportunity to respond. Authors who cannot explain themselves usually find their scholarly reputations ending in tatters.[2]

Scandals are rare, fortunately. Still, questioning evidence choices is probably the most common form that critical thinking takes in sociology. It is always possible to question the choices an author has made in handling evidence. Criticisms of quantitative work often focus on showing how different choices—using different statistical methods, for example, or incorporating additional variables in the analysis—might have led to a different interpretation. Sometimes critics request access to research data (usually in the form of electronic files) so they can conduct their own analyses. In other cases, the original researchers voluntarily make their data available online and invite others to conduct their own examinations—thereby declaring confidence in their findings.

Critiques of qualitative research often focus on evidence as well. In most cases, replication is simply not possible, and even if it is, it would be prohibitively expensive in terms of the time and money required. In any case, the original researchers can always argue that they accurately summarized what they observed. But critics can argue that the researchers misunderstood what they observed, perhaps because their interpretations were shaped by what they expected to find.

Another line of criticism concerns ethics. For instance, sociologists disagree about whether it is ethical to deceive one's research subjects, for example by misrepresenting the topic of the experiment in which they are participating. Sociologists often strive to disguise their research settings by, for instance, renaming the site of their research (such as Muncie, Indiana, becoming "Middletown" or Newburyport, Massachusetts, becoming "Yankee City") and giving individuals pseudonyms. Still, research subjects have been known to complain about the ways they were characterized. And there are concerns that some subjects might have been harmed, even traumatized, by participating in a research project. This has led the American Sociological Association, among other professional organizations, to devise ethical codes for its members, even as universities require that researchers submit their research proposals for approval by the campus human subjects board.

Questions about Research

At bottom, no piece of research is perfect or definitive. Every researcher is forced to make choices: choices about what they want to study (sometimes called the research question); choices about what they will measure and how they will go about measuring; and choices about how they will present and interpret the evidence they produce. Most researchers are well aware that the choices they make are consequential, and many research papers conclude with a call for further research, based on somewhat different choices, to lend support to the presented findings.

No doubt the vast majority of social scientific researchers report their results honestly. Instances of falsified or fabricated results are incredibly rare, and cases of reported plagiarism are also quite uncommon. In the rare instances when these are discovered, they often result in widely publicized scandals, news of which may spread far beyond academia. But dishonesty is only one—relatively unusual—reason to question research.

Every researcher has had to make choices, and at least some of those choices are likely to have affected the research results. So it is always possible for critics to suggest that the results might have been different if the research question had been formulated differently, if some other definition or measurement of the variables had been chosen, or if the analysis had focused on different evidence. It is always possible for reasonable people to disagree, to raise questions, and to start a conversation.

Such conversations can inspire people to think more deeply about research, and to devise other research projects that can help resolve the questions raised by critics.

Critical Thinking Takeaways

- Choices about presenting evidence are inevitable.
- Evidence can be more or less persuasive, and all evidence is potentially subject to challenge.

13 *Echo Chambers*

Chapter 2 made the point that the greatest challenge of critical thinking is to accurately assess our own ideas. This makes sense. It is easy for us to criticize views we disagree with—after all, if we consider them mistaken, we must have some reason for thinking that way, which we should be able to explain. But it is much harder to criticize views we agree with, those we believe are correct. When we are convinced that an idea is valid, we are unlikely to view it all that critically, and we may be suspicious of efforts to criticize it. This tendency be to less critical of our own thinking has real consequences for social scientific research.

Recognizing and Addressing One's Own Biases

Researchers have long recognized the danger of scientists being insufficiently critical of their own ideas. For example, someone who discovers a new medication naturally hopes that it will help patients; even doctors who did not create the medication but who have been chosen to test its effects on their patients are likely to view this innovation with hope; and of course those patients want the drug to help them. But does the new drug work? People invested in—who have high expectations for—a new drug tend to interpret the results of trial treatments positively, to report that it has worked. However, if you introduce a placebo—a pill that contains no active ingredient, so it could not possibly have any effect—but tell doctors and patients that it contains a promising new drug, they often report that this new treatment has indeed helped.[1] Their hopes lead them to imagine that the treatment has been effective.

Researchers' expectations can also distort social science research findings. Imagine a psychology experiment in which researchers are running rats through a maze to test the hypothesis that smarter rats will complete the maze faster. They use two groups of rats: the first group is described as regular old rats, while the second group, they are told, contains rats that have been selectively bred for greater intelligence—they are the offspring of really smart rats. The results are not surprising: those bred-to-be-smarter rats turn out to solve the maze faster than their garden-variety competition. There's just one problem: the two groups of rats were chosen from a collection of genetically identical rats; the claim that one group had been bred for its maze-running intelligence was false. The two groups of rats should have completed the maze in the same amount of time, but the purportedly smarter group that the researchers expected to do better actually outperformed the supposedly ordinary rats.

This is an example of what is called *experimenter effect*.[2] The experimenter expects a certain result, and then gets results in line with those expectations. How does this happen? There are probably lots of reasons. For example, suppose that two rats get equally close to the end of the maze, right on the edge of finishing; the experimenter may be more likely to judge the said-to-be-smarter rat as having come just close enough—by a whisker if you will—to count as having completed the maze first, while the said-to-be-dumber rat is judged to have almost but not quite finished. Knowing what you are supposed to find can influence what you do find.

It is important to appreciate that this does not mean anyone is necessarily doing anything fraudulent or deliberately falsifying their reports. Scandals about research fraud do make the head-lines, but they are rare.[3] Most researchers undoubtedly think they are being conscientious. But expecting to find certain results makes it easy to make judgments consistent with those expectations. Placebos and said-to-be-smarter rat experiments are designed to identify experimenter effects by manipulating the expectations of the research subjects—in these cases, the doctors and patients, or the people running rats through mazes—while holding everything else constant. There is no reason why the placebo or the said-to-be-smarter rats should perform better—unless the subjects' expectations shape the findings.

To be sure, people bring expectations to all sorts of real-world situations, with consequences that may well affect their lives. Perhaps the most dramatic study of experimenter effects involved classroom teachers. First, researchers gave intelligence tests to a group of elementary school students. They then randomly selected about a fifth of the students and told their teachers that those students' performances indicated that they were likely to be "intellectual bloomers" who would show dramatic improvements during the coming year.[4] The result—you can see what's coming—was that the predicted-to-show-improvement group in fact did improve more than the students for whom the teachers were not given positive expectations. Notice that this study was designed to avoid hurting anyone: to the degree that there was an experimenter effect, it served to help some students by encouraging teachers to think better of them. Still, this is a troubling finding. Think for a moment about all the expectations—the assumptions and stereotypes about others, including others' ideas about you—that people carry into all sorts of social situations. What effects do those expectations have?

The tendency for researchers' expectations to shape what they find is a serious problem for all branches of science, and well-designed research projects try to avoid experimenter effects. Medical researchers long ago discovered that doctors who are trying some promising new wonder drug often find that the new drug in fact outperforms the established treatment—if they know which patients are receiving the promising treatment. It is also true that patients who know they are receiving a promising drug will experience improvement. This is why the best clinical drug trials are *double-blind*—that is, neither the patients nor the medical professionals administering the treatments know whether a given patient is receiving the experimental drug or is a member of the control group.

Expectations and Sociologists

The possibility that researchers' expectations can affect what they find reminds us once again that the greatest challenge of critical thinking is to question the ideas that we already believe. All scientists—but especially social scientists—need to be careful to judge their own claims by standards that are at least as rigorous as those they apply to claims with which they disagree.

Most sociological research does not involve formal experiments, which means that sociologists ordinarily cannot rely on double-blind research conditions to foster more accurate findings. As we have seen, sociological research typically begins with the researcher's interest in some social process or setting. Quite often, this interest is rooted in autobiography: the investigator may have experienced or observed something that they found interesting, that they think they might have a sociological explanation for—and so they devise a study. Of course, when the research results are reported, this autobiographical tale tends to be downplayed, even to disappear. Instead, the research report uses dispassionate language and frames the work in terms of a theoretical question that can be addressed through careful, scientific investigation.

This is inevitable. As we have seen, sociologists are insiders—both within the discipline of sociology, which gives them a sense of what other sociologists might find interesting, and within society generally, including within particular groups and settings, which affects what they might consider worthy of study. Often, their insider status gives them a rooting interest in what they uncover: they would prefer that their results reveal what they expect to find, both because it is always nice to have one's hypotheses confirmed and because they feel it should be the correct result. But all of this means that sociologists rarely embark on a research project without expectations. In most cases, they have an idea of what they are likely to find, and a sense of why those results might be valuable. Under these circumstances, researchers need to be especially watchful, ever aware of the possibility that their expectations may skew what they discover. They must do everything they can to ensure that their findings are accurate. Critical thinking is key.

The Complications of Ideological Homogeneity

All of this is complicated by political ideology. We have already noted that contemporary sociologists are relatively politically homogeneous. That is, the vast majority of sociologists locate themselves somewhere on the liberal/progressive/radical left side of the spectrum; relatively few think of themselves as conservatives. This relative unanimity of opinion itself shapes sociologists' expectations. It has other consequences as well, beginning with a tendency toward melodrama.

Melodrama

In the theater, old-fashioned melodramas have simplistic plots that revolve around one-dimensional characters who occupy standardized, formulaic roles—the evil, mustache-twirling villain threatens to victimize the innocent, powerless heroine, who is saved at the last moment by the plucky hero. This can make for crowd-pleasing entertainment; the audience hisses at the villain, cries out to warn the heroine, and cheers the hero. The plots of most modern plays and movies, in contrast, are more sophisticated, involving the actions of better-rounded characters. From Oedipus to Spiderman, heroes are not simply good, but they have flaws, and villains have motivations that go beyond having a simply evil nature. The conflicts are more nuanced, and complex plots encourage more thoughtful audience reactions, so that after the drama has ended the audience can continue to ponder the choices the characters made.

Aspects of melodrama can help us consider some aspects of critical thinking in sociology. First, there is melodrama's simplicity of plots and roles. While sociological theories are more complex, they often are built around central mechanisms or social processes. Thus, rational-choice theories emphasize the role of calculated decisions in social life, while conflict theories emphasize how elites maintain control through various forms of domination.

Similarly, sociological camps built around such theoretical perspectives emphasize the ways in which particular aspects of culture or social structure shape—often in harmful ways—social life. What amount to villainous roles can be assigned to structures or processes such as patriarchy, domination, color-blind racism, or neoliberalism. Because everyone within a camp tends to share the same theoretical assumptions, such declarations are rarely disputed. Common expectations discourage sharp criticism of one another's arguments.

Camps, then, can act as echo chambers, in which people agree with one another and congratulate themselves for being in agreement, much as the melodrama's audience reinforces the action by hissing and cheering. This environment makes it difficult for individuals to think critically about their own views, because they continually have those views reinforced by the colleagues who share them.

This situation is exacerbated by sociology's ideological homogeneity. Camps organized around particular theoretical orientations often share not just a set of concepts, but also a general political perspective that may reinforce the theory. Members of these camps, being in general agreement, thus reaffirm the essential correctness of one another's thinking. This, too, discourages critical inspection of one's own ideas. It is an intellectual version of groupthink.[5]

This does not mean that all sociologists march to the same drumbeat. Members of rival camps often debate and disagree, although open conflict is probably less common than disinterest and inattention. Complaints that sociology lacks a core reflect these dispersed interests. The most prestigious venues for publishing sociological articles have long been the discipline's two principal journals, the *American Sociological Review* and the *American Journal of Sociology;*

for decades, their articles have averaged far more citations (indicating that they have influenced the thinking of other sociologists) than pieces in other sociological journals. One might presume that, to the degree sociology has a core, it is reflected in these journals. Most of the work published in these journals features statistical analyses sufficiently sophisticated that the great majority of sociologists probably cannot fully understand them. Such high-end sociology is less a core, than one more camp. Work appearing in these journals may seem irrelevant to the members of many of the discipline's camps. Once a sociologist has completed graduate training, it is quite possible for members in some camps to never read another article in the discipline's major journals, turning instead to their camps' more specialized journals, so that the work that appears in the discipline's leading journals has little impact on the thinking in many camps. At the same time, at least some sociologists may find themselves tempted to immerse themselves in their camps' theoretical melodramas, and bask in the sense that they agree with everyone else.

Predictability

A second effect of sociology's homogeneous ideological environment is a narrowing of the discipline's approach that leads to predictability. While liberals outnumber conservatives in all social science disciplines, economics, political science, and history all have substantial conservative minorities, creating an atmosphere that allows for more internal debate. When an economist addresses some proposed public policy, for example, we cannot necessarily know in advance whether they are likely to speak in support or opposition. This is because when economists disagree, it is not so much about economic principles as about the degree to which the government should step in to stabilize the economy, with more liberal economists generally supporting a more active government role than their more conservative colleagues. Sociologists, in contrast, have relatively few deep divisions over politics and values. This greater ideological homogeneity makes it easier to predict any given sociologist's stance. As we saw in chapter 7, for instance, Team Structure typically overrules Team Culture, blaming inequality and injustice—and social problems generally—on out-of-balance social structures. Critiques that focus on cultural variables—once common—have become quite rare.

This predictability, however, means that sociology risks being boring. Recall our earlier discussion of sociologists' tendency toward pessimism. Evidence for progress is dismissed; indeed, pointing to such evidence is seen as dangerous, in that it may foster complacency instead of a determination to promote social change. Sociologists commenting on public issues often seem to be scolding the status quo.

That said, sociology does feature intradisciplinary disagreement, particularly between the members of rival camps, who may disparage one another's theoretical models or methodological preferences, and who probably have little interest in topics that are the other camps' substantive focus. On occasion, rivals will be dismissed for being politically conservative, again revealing the ideological homogeneity within sociology. There is a righteous tone to some of this criticism. Members of Team Structure, for instance, write off Team Culture's analyses as a form of blaming the victim and imply that scholars who focus on culture bear some of the responsibility for social injustice.

We might wonder how Team Structure sociologists who are parents translate their professional emphasis into parenting practices. We might suspect that most such parents engage in the sort of intensive parenting practiced by other highly educated, upper-middle-class parents.[6] That is, they probably encourage their kids to study for this week's spelling test, and tell them it is important to get good grades because good grades will help them get into a good college, and a college education will in turn lead to a good job and a secure future. What they probably don't do is assure their kids that that spelling test hardly matters, because they have been born into a privileged social class and their future is secured. If the social structure is all that rigid, why emphasize the importance of success in school?

Thus the predictability of sociological pronouncements. And predictability comes with costs. While the between-camp differences within sociology may seem important to the discipline's members, sociology's ideological homogeneity renders those differences nearly invisible to those outside the discipline. Instead, sociologists are seen as taking predictably liberal positions. And this predictability makes sociology seem boring and makes it easier to ignore what sociologists say.

The Importance of Self-Criticism

Precisely because we know that researchers' expectations can distort what they find, it is important for sociologists to think critically about their own work, to try to ensure that their results haven't been shaped inadvertently by their own expectations. Ideally their colleagues—the scholarly community of sociologists—will help researchers by questioning their work; the path to publication features editor and peer reviewers, gatekeepers whose job is to provide such criticism. However, contemporary sociology's organization into camps, along with the discipline's ideological homogeneity, means that editors and peer reviewers are often sympathetic the authors' assumptions and approaches. While there is nothing to keep these actors from taking their critical responsibilities seriously, it is easy to suspect that these arrangements may fail.

In recent years there have been scandals in which people have submitted articles that are basically gibberish to journals in the social sciences and humanities.[7] Some of those papers were accepted and published, at which point the pranksters gleefully revealed their mischief, to the embarrassment of those who had approved works that made no sense. Such examples suggest that there is room for improving critical rigor.

Critical Thinking Takeaways

- Researchers' expectations can influence what they find.
- Expectations pose particular challenges for sociologists because their audiences tend to be intellectually and ideologically homogeneous.

14 *Tough Topics*

By now it should be apparent that every social scientific argument can be—and probably would benefit from being—subjected to critical thinking. In sociology and related disciplines, arguments tend to appear in published reports about research, and all research involves making choices, including measurement choices, comparison choices, and evidence choices. In all of those cases, critics do well to ask whether the researchers' choices may have shaped or distorted the research findings such that reasonable people should doubt the results.

Such questions are entirely legitimate. Although we sometimes talk as though scientific progress is steady, smooth, and inevitable, the truth is messier. Progress comes in fits and starts. Every scientific discipline's history features episodes that today are viewed as mistakes. In every science, knowledge that was once taken for granted has been overturned, often as new ideas supported by stronger evidence emerged. Critical thinking plays a vital role in this process; it helps steer disciplines toward better understanding of their subject matter by challenging the received wisdom. Such criticisms helps scientists reject some ideas as mistaken or misguided, as intellectual dead ends, while at the same time encouraging more promising alternative lines of thinking.

Those ideas that were eventually discarded had their advocates, people who believed in them and produced research findings that seemed to support them. Spare a moment to consider those who resisted new ideas, and who are now remembered as clinging to mistaken notions. But recognize, too, that resistance to novel thinking and change isn't always wrong. While we remember the dramatic episodes when conventional wisdom was overturned, there have also been plenty of new ideas that didn't pan out—ideas that may have been briefly fashionable, only to fade. In other words, at any given moment both change and the status quo have advocates, and each of these positions may eventually win some of these debates. Over time, evidence should settle which ideas will endure, and which will fade away.

This description is comforting, for it suggests that truth—in the form of superior evidence—wins. It is easy to see things this way in hindsight, when we stand back at a distance from earlier debates. Up close, emotions run higher. Because people are invested in their positions, critical thinking becomes extremely important— especially when it questions widely held ideas.

These processes roil contemporary sociology. In a discipline with considerable ideological homogeneity, agreement can be so widespread that questioning the consensus is discouraged.

Cultural Waves

Culture and social structure change. Better communication spreads ideas rapidly, new technologies alter social arrangements, and long-standing assumptions are toppled. It is easy to see many of these changes as positive. At a global level, more people live in democracies, literacy has spread, fertility rates have fallen, and life expectancies have risen. In the United States, we can point to improved standards of living and expanded rights for women and ethnic and sexual minorities. These developments affect large numbers of people (although never everyone equally or all at once), and while they may be resisted at first, they eventually gain fairly broad-based support and are widely seen as evidence of progress.

We can think of these changes as occurring in broad cultural waves that gain general acceptance. A relatively recent example is the internet: while people may complain about some aspects of the internet, the great majority of people rely on it; it rapidly grew from a novelty to being not just taken for granted, but an essential feature of our lives. It is accepted, and this seems unlikely to change—at least until some superior communications system emerges.

Other developments affect narrower swaths of society—such as sociologists. New concepts, theoretical perspectives, and methodological techniques continually emerge. Some of them find favor and spread relatively widely within the discipline, or at least within individual camps. In many cases, these changes are discipline-specific, in that they have—at least initially—little relevance outside sociology. But it is also the case that changes in the larger society can inspire parallel developments within sociology. For instance, the renewed interest in women's issues in the early 1970s (what was then called the women's liberation movement) led sociologists to focus more closely on what then were termed sex roles, soon to be relabeled gender.

Such developments can generate a great deal of interest and enthusiasm within sociology. Fresh ideas often have many implications; once sociologists adopt the new perspective, they recognize interesting topics that might be explored, leading to all sorts of new research. In some cases—say, with the introduction of a sophisticated statistical technique—the impact may be limited; beyond a single camp, few people may notice what's happening. But in cases where changes in the larger society reach sociology, the effect may be very broad. Thus, the new attention on women's issues in the larger society affected sociologists throughout the discipline—whereas for decades women's issues had been compartmentalized within sociology of the family, those who studied formal organizations now found themselves thinking about women's place in those organizations, sociologists of deviance began focusing on women's experiences as deviants and as victims of deviance, and so on, until soon it was commonplace to view virtually any topic through the lens of gender, and to critique other sociologists' analyses for failing to incorporate gender.

The impact of such cultural waves can be enhanced by sociology's ideological homogeneity. The movements for civil rights, women's rights, and gay and lesbian rights found their greatest support among political liberals. Not surprisingly, they also found strong, widespread support among sociologists whose personal sympathies were aligned with these movements.

Effective cultural waves become taken for granted; it seems unthinkable that society could revert to what are now viewed as antiquated, mistaken practices. (Our anxieties about such a possibility are explored in all those postapocalyptic and dystopian tales about people struggling amid the remnants of collapsed civilizations.) Cultural waves create new assumptions about how things should and will work. They reverberate through society—and through sociology.

Good Guys and Bad Guys

Within sociology, recent cultural waves—especially the campaigns for the rights of various disadvantaged categories of people—have had a profound influence. Social stratification has always been a central sociological concern, but increasingly social structure—social relationships of class, status, race, and gender—is understood as reflecting differences in power. Terms that evoke raw power, such as *elites, exploitation,* and *domination,* appear more often in the sociological literature. Many sociologists take it for granted that their sympathies should be with the less powerful, with those who have been harmed by others' power.

This shift has led many sociologists to focus on victimization and vulnerability, an early expression of which was the idea of blaming the victim.[1] While the phrase was coined by a psychologist, sociologists readily adopted it. Its central idea is that within a society characterized by significant inequality, people with few opportunities often make choices that prove costly, such as dropping out of school, using drugs, or committing crimes, and those choices may leave them even worse off. Conventional society may blame these individuals for their poor choices, but, the argument goes, this blame is misplaced, for these people have been victimized by a society that placed terrible obstacles in their paths. The blame should be redirected at the racist class system that disadvantages so many.

Obviously, sociologists had considerable sympathy for an argument that emphasized the importance of social arrangements. At the same time, a compatible cultural wave arose that drew attention to the social circumstances of victims; these included prominent campaigns against various forms of abuse (such as child abuse and elder abuse); a victim rights movement that sought to provide greater support for victims of rape and other crimes; and the rise of victimology as a specialty within criminology. Talking about victims had become fashionable.

This focus on victims reflects a melodramatic vision (see chapter 13), in which victims are seen as vulnerable, weak, and deserving of understanding and sympathy. Some sociologists seemed to consider blaming the victim a logical fallacy, treating it as an error in reasoning. This is a defensible position, but it should be recognized that it is possible to do sociology based on other assumptions. Sociologists of juvenile delinquency, for example, have described the "good boy problem."[2] That is, it is always possible to point to young men who were raised in difficult circumstances (growing up in a slum, say), the sorts of conditions associated with becoming delinquent, yet who avoided falling prey to delinquency--that is, they were "good boys." In other words, arguing that delinquency is caused by these structural conditions overpredicts: if growing up in slums causes delinquency, how can we explain all those kids from slums who don't become delinquent? If sociologists who argue that blaming the victim ignores the power of social structure, those good boys remind us that that power has limits.

One can point to many analogous examples. A great deal of evidence, for example, shows that a substantial minority of children raised in the poorest quintile (that is, the 20 percent of households with the lowest incomes) wind up remaining in the lowest quintile as adults. The fact that not everyone achieves the American dream and gets ahead is sometimes presented as a telling indictment of the American social system. However, this critique ignores the evidence that most children raised in the bottom quintile *do* move into one of the higher quintiles as adults—those we might think of as the good boys (and girls) of upward mobility. Just as it is possible to exaggerate social structure's power to cause delinquency, social structure's tendency to block mobility can also be overstated.

Team Structure certainly has a point. Individuals' childhood circumstances do make it harder to move far up (or down) the social ladder than to remain where you are. We can imagine lots of reasons for this: obstacles such as discrimination and prejudice may stand in the way of people trying to move up; those from less advantaged backgrounds have less access to resources (good schools, for instance); and individuals tend to plan their lives around circumstances with which they are already familiar. Because many students enter college believing that the United States is an especially open society, one where anyone can "make it to the top," introductory sociology instructors have long viewed it as their responsibility to demonstrate that Americans in fact have less social mobility than students imagine. Tied in with this is the discipline's emphasis on victims and the vulnerable.[3] Yet there is a tension here, for this attitude can lead to ignoring the substantial amount of mobility that actually occurs in spite of all the obstacles.

Focusing on victimization also supports an ever more expansive definition of its nature. Consider the concept of microaggressions.[4] These are, as the word suggests, small moments, words, or gestures, often occurring in face-to-face interaction, that are understood as disparaging another's social position. The concept is most often used in psychiatry, psychology, and education, although some sociologists have adopted it as well. The basic idea is that people can be victimized—made to feel stressed or isolated—by being the target of many small slights. Most often, microaggressions are discussed as involving race or ethnicity, but the concept has been applied to gender, sexuality, and other categories of people deemed vulnerable.

Whether an act can be characterized as a microaggression depends solely on the perception of the victim: a comment that may be intended to be friendly can be classified as a microaggression if it is construed the person to whom it is directed as revealing some underlying bias; as an example, being asked "Where are you from?" might be understood to imply, "You don't belong here."

Like color-blind racism, the idea of microaggression gives analysts the power to identify victimization in circumstances where those being characterized as victimizers may deny that they have any malicious intent.[5] Notice that both terms incorporate words—*racism* and *aggression*—that suggest they should be understood as troubling, harsh behaviors. Of course, sociologists trade on their ability to offer a surprising perspective, to interpret social life in terms different than what their subjects might choose. It is no wonder that the concept has become fashionable. At the same time, the concept's usefulness cannot be taken for granted; like all new ideas in the social sciences, it needs to be the subject of critical thinking.

Ultimately, cultural waves can distort disciplinary thinking, encouraging formulating research questions consistent with the wave's assumptions while failing to attend to other topics that fit less neatly into the wave's portrayal of society and social life. It is easy for ideas to take hold in a camp filled with members who share a particular set of concerns, and not that much more difficult to find those ideas tolerated, if not generally adopted, in an ideologically homogeneous discipline.

Cataloging forms of inequality is an important part of sociology, and of the social sciences more generally. But sociology's mission extends beyond simply decrying inequality, and catching a cultural wave does not justify abandoning the rest of sociology's agenda.

Taboos

But there is another, potentially more serious consequence of disciplinary unanimity. Sociologists may become reluctant to address Research Questions That Must Not Be Asked. That is, there are taboo topics, or at least potentially taboo findings.

In general, these topics address such hot-button issues as race, class, gender, and sexuality. All of these topics have long been studied by sociologists. Early sociological research exposed the harms caused by racial discrimination and the class structure and sought to explain the responses of those victimized by these systems. Interest in inequalities based on gender and sexuality arose somewhat later. In all of these cases, sociologists argued that discrimination was wrong.

At the same time, sociologists sought to document evidence of inequality. And of course, there is plenty of inequality to document. Virtually any social indicator—income, wealth, life expectancy, educational attainment—reveals patterns related to ethnicity, class, gender, or sexuality, and sociologists—most of whom belong to Team Structure—are quite comfortable explaining these patterns as caused by structural arrangements, while dismissing (sometimes out of hand) explanations that propose other causes. And, because there is such ideological unanimity within sociology, it is possible to argue that sociologists should not even ask whether other explanations are relevant.

Consider the relevance of family structure to children's prospects. Political conservatives—who, remember, are rare within sociology—argue that the traditional nuclear family consisting of a married man and woman and their children gives children various advantages. But society has been changing: more children are born to unmarried parents, and more couples split up, so that a larger share of children live in single-parent households; in addition, more children are being raised by gay or lesbian couples. In general, sociologists support these changes that lead to children being raised in diverse households. Many conservatives, however, worry that children from these nontraditional households will be harmed—that they will have problems in school or suffer other sorts of harms.

One might imagine that this would create a research opportunity for sociologists. And it has—but the results, depending on what they show, are not always welcomed. Research that shows that children do well in all sorts of family settings are readily accepted. Research that suggests that children from traditional families have advantages, however, is likely to be met with less enthusiasm. Of course, this is nothing new. Findings that challenge a discipline's current consensus have always faced resistance, some of which undoubtedly reflects disputes about the merits of the research in question.[6] But taboos are different—they foreclose debate by trying to discourage the very expression of some ideas.

Obviously, it is perfectly legitimate to criticize a researcher's measurement, comparison, and evidence choices. In some cases, scientists may feel comfortable dismissing out of hand claims that have been thoroughly debunked—like the idea that the earth is flat. But such dismissal presupposes that there is already established agreement on the evidence for earth-is-round arguments, and the flaws in earth-is-flat claims. This is very different from rejecting research simply because the findings are inconsistent with what one might wish had been found.

Thinking about What's Difficult

Critical thinking is very important because it allows social scientists to build knowledge using the most compelling evidence. Critical thinking also presents challenges because we often think we already know what is true, and we resist—even resent—others' criticisms.

The same standard applies to all sociologists in all their various orientations and camps: if we are trying to understand the world as it is—as opposed to however we might wish it to be—we need to think critically about our own claims, and we also need to listen to and consider others' critiques. This is a messy, often uncomfortable process, but it is essential to building sociological knowledge.

Critical Thinking Takeaways

- The development of new knowledge is often controversial and contentious.
- Cultural waves shape our openness to different ideas.
- Defining topics as taboo discourages critical thinking.

Afterword

Why Critical Thinking Is Important

Critical thinking can be a lonely pursuit. After all, it involves being critical—of other people's ideas, but also of one's own reasoning. It isn't much fun to be criticized; it can be very frustrating. It is almost always easier to gloss over critical thinking.

Yet critical thinking is extremely important. Progress comes from a willingness to think carefully, to question what you're told, to be skeptical about received wisdom. Look around yourself; even as you read this, you are surrounded by objects, and your head is filled with ideas, that are the products of scientific progress—that is, of critical thinking. Critical thinking has gotten humanity where it is today, and it is vitally necessary if things are going to continue getting better.

Notes

Chapter 1. What Is Critical Thinking?

1. The critical thinking literature is vast. The ERIC (Education Resources Information Center) database—the basic resource for searching education scholarship—lists thousands of sources that mention critical thinking in their abstracts.

2. At the same time, a common criticism of our schools and colleges is that too many students don't acquire the critical thinking skills they need. For example, consider Arum and Roksa's disturbing finding that "three semesters of college education . . . have a barely noticeable impact on students' skills in critical thinking . . . " (2011, 35).

3. Merseth (1993).

4. Neem (2019) argues that the most important critical thinking skills are discipline-specific: that is, historians, literary scholars, chemists, and sociologists, for example, require different sorts of skills.

Chapter 2. The Basics: Arguments and Assumptions

1. I've borrowed the grounds-warrants-conclusions model of arguments from Stephen Toulmin (1958).

Chapter 3. Everyday Arguments

1. Kohler-Hausmann (2007) discusses how stories about "welfare queens" shaped debates on welfare policy.

2. See, for example, National Center for Statistics and Analysis (2018).

3. Latin terminology—for example, post hoc ergo propter hoc (the error of assuming that if B follows A, A must have caused B)—fills the traditional catalog of logical fallacies. This book will focus on those that seem particularly relevant to sociology.

4. Scherker (2015); Brown (2015).

5. S. Davis (2015); Gilson (2013).

6. For one review of the issues and evidence related to abortion safety, see National Academies of Sciences, Engineering, and Medicine (2018).

7. On metaphors' importance, see Lakoff and Johnson (1980). For sociological critiques of particular metaphors, see Best (2018) and Furedi (2018).

8. There is a large literature. For instance, see Zygmunt (1970).

9. For instance, see Collins (2000).

Chapter 4. The Logic of Social Science

1. The eighteenth-century philosopher David Hume is credited with first articulating the basic criteria for judging causal arguments.

2. Becker (1963), 135–46.

3. Dickson (1968), 153 n33.

4. For other examples of this problem, see Fischer (1970), 169–72.

5. Robin (2004).

6. Laposata, Kennedy, and Glantz (2014).

Chapter 5. Authority and Social Science Arguments

1. Shiller (2015).

2. Best (2003).

3. Best (2001a).

4. Sociologists sometimes study the workings of their own discipline— what is called the sociology of sociology. There is even a journal devoted to the topic, *The American Sociologist*.

Chapter 6. Sociology as a Social World

1. Pease and Rytina (1968); also Best (2016).

2. See Gubrium and Holstein's (1997) discussion of "methods talk."

3. Best (2006a).

4. For decades, studies of professors' political orientations have consistently found that sociology is among the disciplines with the highest proportions of liberals and/or Democrats. For twenty-first century examples, see Cardiff and Klein (2005); Gross and Simmons (2014).

5. Since I am categorizing sociologists, it is probably fair that I reveal a bit about where I fit in sociology's world. Like most sociologists, I think of myself as politically liberal. My principal sociological camps are theoretical (symbolic interactionism) and substantive (studies of social problems construction).

6. Cole (1994, 2006).

Chapter 7. Orientations

1. Pinker (2018).

2. Although not a sociologist, Diamond (2005) offers case studies of collapse.

3. Herman (1997).

4. For example, see Lareau (2011).

5. Goffman (1952). For a detailed analysis of Goffman's comic style in his classic book *Asylums,* see Fine and Martin (1990).

6. M. Davis (1993), 150.

7. For example, Brooks (2000). On Wolfe, see Best (2001b).

8. Parkinson (1957); Peter and Hull (1969).

Chapter 8. Words

1. Best (2003).

2. There are many examples, but the classic critiques are Mills (1959) and Sorokin (1956).

3. Becker (1986).

4. Billig (2013).

5. Smith (1992).

6. Best (2006b).

7. These are not new issues. Allport (1954) considered failing to capitalize *Negro* problematic.

8. Goffman (1961).

9. Furedi (2016); Haslam et al. (2020).

10. Goffman (1961), 4 (emphasis in the original).

Chapter 9. Questions and Measurements

1. Mosher, Miethe, and Phillips (2002).

2. Mosher, Miethe, and Phillips (2002).

3. Lee (2007).

4. This is a short book that deals with a broad topic, so it inevitably glosses over lots of particulars. Other authors offer more detailed guidelines for questioning pieces of research (e.g., Harris [2014]; Nardi [2017]; Ogden [2019]), and there is a vast literature on social scientific methodology.

Chapter 10. Variables and Comparison

1. On the various ways pharmaceutical companies sponsoring research into the value of their products can shape the scientific literature, see Goldacre (2012).

2. The classic statement of this logic appears in Glaser and Strauss (1967).

Chapter 11. Tendencies

1. Selvin (1958) coined this term, although he credits the idea to an earlier paper by Robinson (1950).

2. For example, Buckingham, Comen, and Suneson (2018).

3. Federal Bureau of Investigation (2018).

Chapter 12. Evidence

1. Eisner (2003).

2. Robin (2004).

Chapter 13. Echo Chambers

1. Harrington (1997).

2. Rosenthal (1966).

3. Robin (2004).

4. Rosenthal and Jacobson (1968).

5. Janis (1982).

6. Lareau (2011).

7. For the pranksters' accounts of these events, see Pluckrose, Lindsay, and Boghossian (2018); and Sokal and Bricmont (1998).

Chapter 14. Tough Topics

1. Ryan (1971).

2. Reckless, Dinitz, and Murray (1957). This term originated, of course, before sociologists began trying to eradicate sexism from their language.

3. Waiton (2019).

4. Embrick, Domínguez, and Karsak (2017).

5. Bonilla-Silva (2015).

6. Redding (2013).

References

Allport, Gordon W. 1954. *The Nature of Prejudice*. Cambridge, MA: Addison-Wesley.

Arum, Richard, and Josipa Roksa. 2011. *Academically Adrift: Limited Learning on College Campuses*. Chicago: University of Chicago Press.

Becker, Howard S. 1963. *Outsiders: Studies in the Sociology of Deviance*. New York: Free Press.

———. 1986. *Writing for Social Scientists: How to Start and Finish Your Thesis, Book, or Article*. Chicago: University of Chicago Press.

Best, Joel. 2001a. "Giving It Away: The Ironies of Sociology's Place in Academia." *American Sociologist* 32, 1: 107–13.

———. 2001b. "'Status! Yes!': Tom Wolfe as a Sociological Thinker." *American Sociologist* 32, 4: 5–22.

———. 2003. "Killing the Messenger: The Social Problems of Sociology." *Social Problems* 50, 1: 1–13.

———. 2006a. "Blumer's Dilemma: The Critic as a Tragic Figure." *American Sociologist* 37, 3: 5–14.

———. 2006b. *Flavor of the Month: Why Smart People Fall for Fads*. Berkeley: University of California Press.

———. 2016. "Following the Money across the Landscape of Sociology Journals." *American Sociologist* 47, 2–3: 158–73.

———. 2018. *American Nightmares: Social Problems in an Anxious World*. Oakland: University of California Press.

Billig, Michael. 2013. *Learn to Write Badly: How to Succeed in the Social Sciences*. Cambridge: Cambridge University Press.

Bonilla-Silva, Eduardo. 2015. "The Structure of Racism in Color-Blind, 'Post Racial' America." *American Behavioral Scientist* 59, 11: 1358–76.

Brooks, David. 2000. *Bobos in Paradise: The New Upper Class and How They Got There.* New York: Simon & Schuster.

Brown, Kristi Burton. 2015. "10 Pro-Abortion Myths That Need To Be Completely Debunked." *LifeNews.com,* February 25, www.lifenews .com/2015/02/25/10-pro-abortion-myths-that-need-to-be-completely-debunked.

Buckingham, Cheyenne, Evan Comen, and Grant Suneson. 2018. "America's Most and Least Educated States." *MSN.Money,* September 24, www.msn .com/en-us/money/personalfinance/america's-most-and-least-educated-states/ar-BBNlBSS.

Cardiff, Christopher F., and Daniel B. Klein. 2005. "Faculty Partisan Affiliations in All Disciplines: A Voter-Registration Study." *Critical Review* 17, 3: 237–55.

Cole, Stephen. 1994. "Why Sociology Doesn't Make Progress Like the Natural Sciences." *Sociological Forum* 9, 2: 133–54.

———. 2006. "Disciplinary Knowledge Revisited: The Social Construction of Sociology." *American Sociologist* 37, 2: 41–56.

Collins, H.M. 2000. "Surviving Closure: Post-Rejection Adaptation and Plurality in Science." *American Sociological Review* 65, 6: 824–45.

Davis, Murray S. 1993. *What's So Funny? The Comic Conception of Culture and Society.* Chicago: University of Chicago Press.

Davis, Sean. 2015. "7 Gun Control Myths That Just Won't Die." *The Federalist. com,* October 7, http://thefederalist.com/2015/10/07/7-gun-control-myths-that-just-wont-die.

Diamond, Jared. 2005. *Collapse: How Societies Choose to Fail or Succeed.* New York: Viking.

Dickson, Donald T. 1968. "Bureaucracy and Morality: An Organizational Perspective on a Moral Crusade." *Social Problems* 16, 2: 143–56.

Eisner, Manuel. 2003. "Long-Term Historical Trends in Violent Crime." *Crime and Justice* 30: 83–142.

Embrick, David G., Silvia Domínguez, and Baran Karsak. 2017. "More Than Just Insults: Rethinking Sociology's Contribution to Scholarship on Racial Microaggressions." *Sociological Inquiry* 87, 2: 193–206.

Federal Bureau of Investigation. 2018. *2017 Hate Crime Statistics,* Table 12. Available at https://ucr.fbi.gov/hate-crime/2017/topic-pages/tables /table-12.xls.

Fine, Gary Alan, and Daniel D. Martin. 1990. "A Partisan View: Sarcasm, Satire, and Irony as Voices in Erving Goffman's *Asylums.*" *Journal of Contemporary Ethnography* 19, 1: 89–115.

Fischer, David Hackett. 1970. *Historians' Fallacies: Toward a Logic of Historical Thought.* New York: Harper & Row.

Furedi, Frank. 2016. "The Cultural Underpinning of Concept Creep." *Psychological Inquiry* 27, 1: 34–39.

———. 2018. *How Fear Works: Culture of Fear in the Twenty-First Century.* London: Bloomsbury Continuum.

Gilson, Dave. 2013. "10 Pro-Gun Myths, Shot Down. *Mother Jones.com,* January 31, www.motherjones.com/politics/2013/01/pro-gun-myths-fact-check.

Glaser, Barney G., and Anselm L. Strauss. 1967. *The Discovery of Grounded Theory: Strategies for Qualitative Research.* Chicago: Aldine.

Goffman, Erving. 1952. "On Cooling the Mark Out: Some Aspects of Adaptation to Failure." *Psychiatry* 15, 4: 451–63.

———. 1961. *Asylums: Essays on the Social Situation of Mental Patients and Other Inmates.* Garden City, NY: Doubleday Anchor.

Goldacre, Ben. 2012. *Bad Pharma: How Drug Companies Mislead Doctors and Harm Patients.* London: Fourth Estate.

Gross, Neil, and Solon Simmons. 2014. "The Social and Political Views of American College and University Professors." In *Professors and Their Politics,* ed. Neil Gross and Solon Simmons, 19–49. Baltimore, MD: Johns Hopkins University Press.

Gubrium, Jaber F., and James A. Holstein. 1997. *The New Language of Qualitative Method.* New York: Oxford University Press.

Harrington, Anne, ed. 1997. *The Placebo Effect: An Interdisciplinary Explora-tion.* Cambridge, MA: Harvard University Press.

Harris, Scott R. 2014. *How to Critique Journal Articles in the Social Sciences.* Thousand Oaks, CA: Sage.

Haslam, Nick, Brodie C. Dakin, Fabian Fabiano, Melanie J. McGrath, Joshua Rhee, Ekaterina Vylomova, Morgan Weaving, and Melissa A. Wheeler.

2020. "Harm Inflation: Making Sense of Concept Creep." *European Review of Social Psychology* 31, 1: 254–86.

Herman, Arthur. 1997. *The Idea of Decline in Western History.* New York: Simon & Schuster.

Janis, Irving L. 1982. *Groupthink: Psychological Studies of Policy Decisions and Fiascoes.* Boston: Houghton Mifflin.

Kohler-Hausmann, Julilly. 2007. "'The Crime of Survival': Fraud Prosecutions, Community Surveillance, and the Original 'Welfare Queen.'" *Journal of Social History* 41, 2: 329–54.

Lakoff, George, and Mark Johnson. 1980. *Metaphors We Live By.* Chicago: University of Chicago Press.

Laposata, Elizabeth, Allison P. Kennedy, and Stanton A. Glantz. 2014. "When Tobacco Targets Direct Democracy." *Journal of Health Politics, Policy, and Law* 39, 3: 537–64.

Lareau, Annette. 2011. *Unequal Childhoods: Class, Race, and Family Life.* 2nd ed. Berkeley: University of California Press.

Lee, Murray. 2007. *Inventing Fear of Crime: Criminology and the Politics of Anxiety.* Cullompton, Devon, UK: Willan.

Merseth, Katherine K. 1993. "How Old Is the Shepherd? An Essay about Mathematics Education." *Phi Delta Kappan* 74 (March): 548–54.

Mills, C. Wright. 1959. *The Sociological Imagination.* New York: Oxford University Press.

Mosher, Clayton J., Terance D. Miethe, and Dretha M. Phillios. 2002. *The Mismeasure of Crime.* Thousand Oaks, CA: Sage.

Nardi, Peter M. 2017. *Critical Thinking: Tools for Evaluating Research.* Oakland: University of California Press.

National Academies of Sciences, Engineering, and Medicine. 2018. *The Safety and Quality of Abortion Care in the United States.* Washington, DC: National Academies Press. Available at http://nationalacademies.org/hmd/reports/2018/the-safety-and-quality-of-abortion-care-in-the-united-states.aspx.

National Center for Statistics and Analysis. 2018. *2017 Fatal Motor Vehicle Crashes: Overview.* Traffic Safety Facts Research Note. Report No. DOT HS 812 603. Washington, DC: National Highway Traffic Safety Administration.

Neem, Johann N. 2019. "On Critical Thinking: We Can Only Think Critically about Things about Which We Have Knowledge." *Hedgehog Review Blog,* August 13, https://hedgehogreview.com/blog/thr/posts/on-critical-thinking.

Ogden, Jane. 2019. *Thinking Critically about Research: A Step-by-Step Approach.* New York: Routledge.

Parkinson, C. Northcote. 1957. *Parkinson's Law, and Other Studies in Administration.* Boston: Houghton Mifflin.

Pease, John, and Rytina, Joan. 1968. "Sociology Journals." *American Sociologist* 3, 1: 41–45.

Peter, Laurence J., and Raymond Hull. 1969. *The Peter Principle: Why Things Always Go Wrong.* New York: Morrow.

Pinker, Steven. 2018. *Enlightenment Now: The Case for Reason, Science, Humanism, and Progress.* New York: Viking.

Pluckrose, Helen, James A. Lindsay, and Peter Boghossian. 2018. "Academic Grievance Studies and the Corruption of Scholarship." *Areo,* October 2, https://areomagazine.com/2018/10/02/academic-grievance-studies-and-the-corruption-of-scholarship.

Reckless, Walter C., Siom Dinitz, and Ellen Murray. 1957. "The 'Good Boy' in the High Delinquency Area." *Journal of Criminal Law, Criminology, and Police Science* 48, 1: 18–25.

Redding, Richard E. 2013. "Politicized Science." *Society* 50, 5: 439–46.

Robin, Ron. 2004. *Scandals and Scoundrels: Seven Cases That Shook the Academy.* Berkeley: University of California Press.

Robinson, W. S. 1950. "Ecological Correlations and the Behavior of Individuals." *American Sociological Review* 15, 10: 351–57.

Rosenthal, Robert. 1966. *Experimenter Effects in Behavioral Research.* New York: Appleton-Century-Crofts.

Rosenthal, Robert, and Lenore Jacobson. 1968. *Pygmalion in the Classroom: Teacher Expectations and Pupils' Intellectual Development.* New York: Holt, Rinehart & Winston.

Ryan, William. 1971. *Blaming the Victim.* New York: Pantheon.

Scherker, Amanda. 2015. "10 Abortion Myths That Need to Be Busted." *Huffington Post,* January 22, www.huffingtonpost.com/2015/01/13/abortion-myths_n_6465904.html.

Selvin, Hanan C. 1958. "Durkheim's *Suicide* and Problems of Empirical Research." *American Journal of Sociology* 63, 6: 607–19.

Shiller, Robert J. 2015. *Irrational Exuberance.* 3rd ed. Princeton, NJ: Princeton University Press.

Smith, Tom W. 1992. "Changing Racial Labels: From 'Colored' to 'Negro' to 'Black' to 'African American.'" *Public Opinion Quarterly* 56, 4: 496–514.

Sokal, Alan, and Jean Bricmont. 1998. *Fashionable Nonsense: Postmodern Intellectuals' Abuse of Science.* New York: Picador USA.

Sorokin, Pitirim. 1956. *Fads and Foibles in Modern Sociology and Related Sciences.* Chicago: Regnery.

Toulmin, Stephen Edelston. 1958. *The Uses of Argument.* Cambridge: Cambridge University Press.

Waiton, Stuart. 2019. "The Vulnerable Subject." *Societies* 9: 66.

Zygmunt, Joseph F. 1970. "Prophetic Failure and Chiliastic Identity: The Case of Jehovah's Witnesses." *American Journal of Sociology* 75, 6: 926–48.

Index

abortion, 21–22, 86
ad hominem arguments, 18–21, 58
anecdotes, 14–18, 63, 113
aphorisms, 23–24
arguments, 8–13, 29; everyday, 14–27
assumptions, 11–12
authority, 39–40, 43, 45, 85
autobiography, sociology as, 69–70, 132

Becker, Howard S., 30
alaming the victim. *See* victimization

camps, 47–52, 58, 74, 77–79, 94–95, 104, 125, 135–37, 139, 147
causality, 29–34, 97
census, 54, 94
choices, 57–58, 89–92, 94, 97, 108, 119–21, 126–28, 140, 149
citations, 81, 125, 127, 136
claims, 2–3, 8–9
class, 99–100
comedy, 70–72
community, 63–64
comparison, 65, 96–108

concept creep, 81–84
conclusions, 8, 10–13
core, 58, 135
crime, measuring, 92–93, 115–16, 123–24
critical, meanings, 1
critical thinking, 1–9, 12
culture. *See* Team Culture

Davis, Murray S., 71–72
decline, 62–63
definitions, 22, 79–84
deviance, 79–82
double-blind, 132

echo chambers, 129–39
ecological fallacy, 114–17
economics, 41–43, 136–37
education, and critical thinking, 1, 4–6; and income, 5
enlightenment, 3–4
envy, 53–58; philosophy, 55–57, 77; physics, 53–56; protest, 57
everyday reasoning, 14–27
evidence, 3–4, 17–18, 25, 34–37,

119–28; effective, 120–23;
not-so-effective, 123–26
experimenter effect, 130–32

facts, 24–26, 39
fads, word, 76–79
fallacies, logical, 11, 19, 75, 154n3
(ch. 3). *See also* ecological fallacy
folk wisdom, 23

gatekeepers, 50–51, 138
gender, 142–43
generalizations, 112
Goffman, Erving, 71, 82–83
good boy problem, 145
grounds, 8–13
groupthink, 135
gun control, 21

hate crimes, 115–16
homogeneity, ideological, 133–39,
141, 143

iceberg tips; 23–24
insiders, 69–70, 74, 96, 133

jargon, 44, 56, 74–76
journals, 47, 49–54, 101–3, 135–36

liberalism, and sociology, 1, 44, 57,
63, 68, 134, 136–38, 143, 155n4
(ch. 6). *See also* homogeneity,
ideological
logic, 10–11

marijuana, 30–31
measurement, 87–95, 99, 114, 121, 124
melodrama, 134–36, 145

metaphors, 23–24
methods, 37, 49–55, 88–91, 99–100
microaggressions, 146–47
Moynihan, Daniel Patrick, 25
myths, 20–23

narratives, 17–18
negative results, 101–2
nonspuriousness, 32–34
nostalgia, 63

Occam's razor, 33
opinions, 39
optimism, 61–62, 64
oOrientations, 61, 72
outcomes, research, 100–4
outsiders, 69–70, 74

patterned variation, 31–32, 110–14
patterns, 28–29, 107
peer review, 51–52, 94–95, 138–39
pessimism, 62–64
placebo, 130–31
polling, 89–91, 104–05, 119–20
poverty, 66–68
precedence, 29–31
predictability, 136–38
probability, 111–12
professional associations, 49–50
progress, 61–63, 137, 140, 142, 151
psychology, 41–43
publication, 47, 49–50

qualitative research, 49, 105–8, 120,
126–27
questions: empirical, 87–89;
sociological, 85–87

rationale, 32
reliability, 89
replication, 35–36, 104–5, 108, 122, 126–27
rhetoric, 10

sample, representative, 89–90
scandals, 35, 126, 128, 131, 139
significance, statistical, 54–55, 117
specialties, 48, 50, 87
social sciences, 6–7, 28, 40–41, 46
social structure. *See* Team Structure
social worlds, 43, 45–46
sociology, 6–7, 41, 43–58, 60
saboos, 148–49

Team Culture, 64–69, 137
Team Structure, 64–69, 137–38, 148

tendencies, 110–18
theoretical schools, 49–51, 55–57, 103, 134–35
Toulmin, Stephen, 10
traffic fatalities, 16–17
tragedy, 70–72
truth, 3

validity, 89
values, 9–10, 86–87
variables, 97–99; dependent, 97; independent, 97; intervening, 98–99, 105, 108, 113–14, 118
variation, explained, 117
victimization, 144–47

warrants, 8–13, 86
waves, cultural, 141–44, 147

Founded in 1893,
UNIVERSITY OF CALIFORNIA PRESS
publishes bold, progressive books and journals
on topics in the arts, humanities, social sciences,
and natural sciences—with a focus on social
justice issues—that inspire thought and action
among readers worldwide.

The UC PRESS FOUNDATION
raises funds to uphold the press's vital role
as an independent, nonprofit publisher, and
receives philanthropic support from a wide
range of individuals and institutions—and from
committed readers like you. To learn more, visit
ucpress.edu/supportus.